"I am asked again and again by lovers of Narnia if there is a book out there that will help them understand the deeper Christian meanings of *The Chronicles of Narnia*. I am happy to say that much desired book now exists. Will Vaus' *The Hidden Story of Narnia* offers a clear and concise analysis of the spiritual architecture that undergirds each of the *Chronicles*, and it does so in a language that should prove equally challenging and accessible to academics, non-academics, college and high school students, and even well-read children. Vaus makes clear all the links between Aslan and Christ and between the Narnia books and the Bible. But he goes far beyond this. He also links the themes of the Narnia books to the vast corpus of Lewis' other works so as to make clear the unity of Lewis' Christian worldview. He further challenges his readers to see and wrestle with the greater moral and ethical dimensions of the Chronicles, highlighting the nature of virtue and vice in a manner that would surely have gained Lewis' hearty approval. He concludes by laying down seven guidelines for living like a Narnian that are practical without being didactic and that will help his readers to carry the message of Narnia into their own lives."

    Louis Markos, Professor in English and Scholar in Residence
    at Houston Baptist University
    Author of *Lewis Agonistes* and *The Life and Writings of C. S. Lewis*

"*The Hidden Story of Narnia* splendidly connects all seven of the Narnia books with not only their biblical correspondences but also with relevant passages from Lewis' other works, allowing readers to journey further up and further in with their understanding of and their appreciation for this great writer and thinker."

    Devin Brown, Professor of English at Asbury University
    Author of *Inside the Voyage of the Dawn Treader*

"Once again, Will Vaus proves himself a wise and trusty guide to C. S. Lewis. Drawing on the full range of Lewis' works and on his biblical, literary, and philosophical sources, this volume is an ideal companion for individual readers or discussion groups that are concerned with the spiritual implications of *The Chronicles of Narnia* and are seeking to understand more fully what it means to 'live like a Narnian.'"

    Sanford Schwartz, Pennsylvania State University
    and author of *C. S. Lewis on the Final Frontier*

"As with his previous work on C. S. Lewis, Will Vaus provides clarity and informed perspective, taking us behind the scenes of the origins and meaning of Narnia. The teacher as well as the student of Narnia will find this a very useful volume."

    Dr. Bruce L. Edwards
    Editor of *C. S. Lewis: Life, Works, Legacy*, 4 vols. (Praeger, 2007)

"What a delightful – and helpful – book! Readers of Lewis' Narnia books will enjoy splashing back into the stories and thinking about the enduring truths so freshly evoked by Lewis and highlighted by Will Vaus. Though rooted in solid scholarship and theology, *The Hidden Story of Narnia* is accessible to those new to both. It will take you back to *The Chronicles of Narnia* for another look – at the books, at yourself."

    Wayne Martindale
    Professor of English, Wheaton College

"C. S. Lewis will continue to be read for a long, long time. He always attracts new readers longing for clear and illuminating introductions to his books, his ideas, and his wide world so integrated by his faith. Will Vaus has proved once again that he knows his subject and he knows how to give readers a more robust appreciation of Lewis. *The Hidden Story of Narnia*, with its clarity and engaging style, is another brilliant example of Vaus' skill as an expositor."

    Jerry Root
    Co-editor of *The Quotable Lewis*

"A thoughtful and thought-provoking book."

    Owen A. Barfield, grandson of one of C. S. Lewis' best friends

"*The Hidden Story of Narnia* gives us a wonderful link between the themes of *The Chronicles of Narnia* and Scripture, both Old and New Testaments. The author is deeply familiar with a broad variety of Lewis' other writings, and adds a lot of depth to the fiction, rooting it in the soil of his more serious material. The questions at the end of each chapter also provide a good springboard for discussion as well as inspiration for personal reflection."

    Laurence Krieg, one of C. S. Lewis' child correspondents

THE HIDDEN STORY OF
NARNIA
A BOOK-BY-BOOK GUIDE TO
C. S. LEWIS' SPIRITUAL THEMES

WILL VAUS

The Hidden Story of Narnia
Copyright © 2010 Will Vaus

Published by Winged Lion Press
Cheshire, CT

All rights reserved. Except in the case of quotations embodied in critical articles or reviews, no part of this book may be reproduced or transmitted in any form or by any means, electronic or mechanical, including photocopying, recording, or by any information storage or retrieval system, without written permission of the publisher.
For information, contact Winged Lion Press www.WingedLionPress.com

Unless otherwise noted Scripture references are taken from
the HOLY BIBLE, NEW INTERNATIONAL VERSION ®.
Copyright © 1973, 1978, 1984 International Bible Society.
Used by permission of Zondervan. All rights reserved.

Winged Lion Press titles may be purchased for business or promotional use or special sales.

10-9-8-7-6-5-4-3-2-1

WINGED LION PRESS

ISBN-13 978-1-936294-02-2

Dedicated to Becky
who is as
Forgiving as Polly
Gentle as Susan
Valiant as Lucy
Brave as Aravis
Persevering as Jill

Contents

	Preface	i
	Introduction	1
I.	*The Magician's Nephew* Creation & Fall	7
II.	*The Lion, the Witch and the Wardrobe* Crucifixion & Resurrection	24
III.	*The Horse and His Boy* Calling & Conversion	37
IV.	*Prince Caspian* Restoring True Religion after a Corruption	53
V.	*The Voyage of the Dawn Treader* The Spiritual Life	68
VI.	*The Silver Chair* War against the Powers of Darkness	87
VII.	*The Last Battle* The Coming of the Antichrist, the End of the World, and the Last Judgment	102
	Conclusion: How to Live Like a Narnian	118
	Bibliography	125
	Index	128
	Acknowledgements	131

Preface

When I was around ten years old, I used to enjoy the family's weekly trip to the local public library. It was there that I discovered C. S. Lewis' Narnia stories, which I have loved ever since. They are cracking stories, written in a loving way, but there was something else indefinable that drew me to them.

The Silver Chair has always been my favorite Narnia story, containing my favorite character (apart from Aslan) – Puddleglum the Marsh-wiggle. At the end of the story when Prince Caspian lies dead in a stream, the Lion weeps tears "more precious than the Earth would be if it was a single solid diamond." To me this speaks of the love of God. Aslan brings Caspian back to life with a drop of his blood. But there was something that I was puzzled about.

Eustace says, "Hasn't he—er—died?" And Aslan replies, "Yes, he has died. Most people have, you know. Even I have. There are very few who haven't." It was this "most people have died" that I didn't understand. I remember asking my father who suggested that I write and ask the author which is exactly what I did.

Some months later my mother came into my bedroom saying, "Anne, I think you've got a letter from C. S. Lewis." I can't tell you how thrilled I was although I have to say that he didn't answer my question properly. He explained about Aslan's death, rather than the "most people". Thinking about it now I think what he meant was that most people who have lived since the time of Adam have died, rather than those who are living now.

Anyway, I was not too worried about that because he explained a lot of other things that I never thought to ask! There was a "deeper meaning" behind those stories that I had loved so much: the story of Christ. I showed this letter to lots of people: family, friends, teachers, vicars, etc. But it wasn't until it got into the hands of Douglas Gresham that people started to really take notice of it. And I, who do not like being in the limelight, found myself something of a celebrity!

Again, I had something of a surprise to receive an email from Mr. Vaus who asked me if I would read the manuscript of his book *The Hidden Story of Narnia*. Amazingly to me, this book uses my letter as the outline. As soon as I started reading I knew I was in for a treat. Will Vaus has the same gift of clarity as Mr. Lewis. Using the Bible and other Lewis books, he has gone into some depth to examine this "deeper meaning". However, this is not simply a study book. He has managed to retain what I call "the Dancing Lawn" factor—the sheer joy and merriment of Lewis' style. When I finished reading the book I felt like all the missing pieces of a jigsaw puzzle had simply fallen into place.

The book ends with an all-important chapter explaining to the readers that Narnia is not inaccessible; and Mr. Vaus shows how we can all live like Narnians. *The Hidden Story of Narnia* shows how *The Chronicles of Narnia* can be, not simply a wonderful set of stories, but the beginning of an even better story, one "which goes on forever: in which every chapter is better than the one before".

> Anne Waller Jenkins
> Hertfordshire, England
> March 2010

Introduction

I lived in Narnia.

Now before you think either: (1) I'm crazy or (2) ask how you can get to Narnia too . . . let me explain.

For the better part of a year my family and I lived in a house called The Narnia Cottage. The place I speak of was actually in the lush, green countryside of Ireland. It was a four hundred year old cottage situated on the twenty-acre estate of Douglas Gresham, the step-son of C. S. Lewis. During that year I worked as Doug's assistant and it was an exciting time indeed. That was the year when Doug was flying back and forth to New Zealand during the filming of *The Lion, the Witch and the Wardrobe*.

Living in the Narnia Cottage and hearing Doug's glowing reports from the movie set were not the only things which made us feel like we were living in Narnia. During that year I read aloud all seven of *The Chronicles of Narnia* to my three boys. Visiting castles, climbing on stone tables, and trying on real armor (all things one can do in Ireland) really helped my children live in the imaginative world which C. S. Lewis created. In fact, every day we walked the hills of Eire we were, in a sense, stomping on Narnian turf, for as many people know, Lewis based the landscape of Narnia on the experience of his own native country.

Though I only lived in the Narnia Cottage for less than a year it would be true to say that I have been living in Narnia imaginatively for about forty years. That's how long ago I was introduced to C. S. Lewis' creation. The wardrobe door was opened for me when my fourth grade teacher read *The Lion, the Witch and the Wardrobe* to our class. By the end of the first chapter, and she read a chapter each day, I was there. I was feeling the crunch of snow underfoot. I was gazing at the glow from the lamppost. I was having tea with Mr. Tumnus, fish and chips with Mr. and Mrs. Beaver. I was living in Narnia, and perhaps have been ever since.

This book began, in a formal sense, during my time living in The Narnia Cottage. However, my insights into the spiritual meaning of Narnia have been gleaned over the past forty years of repeated journeys into these seven fantastic stories.

Hunting for the spiritual themes in Narnia should not be one's first approach to these books. Rather they should be read for the sheer love of the story itself. But having loved the story I have found myself going back to these books over and over again. And each time I read them I see *further up and further in* to their meaning.

How Narnia Came To Be

The Chronicles of Narnia are among the most popular children's stories of all time. They have sold over 100 million copies in 41 languages. These stories were written by an unlikely author of children's books, the bachelor Oxford don, C. S. Lewis. Why did Lewis – tutor, literary critic, and author of numerous books of Christian theology – suddenly turn, in his late 40s, to writing a series of fairy tales? Lewis himself described the eventuality of Narnia by saying that he started writing fairy tales because fairy tales were the best art form for what he wanted to say.[1] Lewis said that this form compelled him to leave out certain things he wanted to leave out, and checked the *expository demon* in him.[2]

---

[1] Lewis, C. S., *On Stories: and Other Essays on Literature,* San Diego: Harcourt Brace & Company, 1982, pp. 46-47. See also Hooper, Walter and Lewis, W. H., eds., *Letters of C. S. Lewis,* San Diego: Harcourt Brace & Company, 1993, [2 December 1962] p. 506.

[2] *On Stories,* p. 37.

Lewis makes it quite clear that he did not begin with the idea of trying to communicate Christianity to children. Rather, the stories began with pictures in his mind – of a faun carrying an umbrella and parcels in a snowy wood, a queen on a sledge, and a magnificent lion. Then the Christian element pushed its way in. Lewis says he began to see how, through a fairy tale, he could sneak past the inhibitions that can paralyze children with regard to Christ.

In his own childhood Lewis found it difficult to love God, or feel appropriately toward the sufferings of Christ, because he was always told how to feel.[3] Rather than telling how, the Narnia stories elicit certain feelings in children. Thus children naturally fall in love with Aslan upon reading about him. In fact, Lewis wrote to one mother because her son, Laurence, was concerned that he loved Aslan more than Jesus. Lewis explained that the boy couldn't love Aslan more than Jesus because the things he loved Aslan for doing or saying were simply the same kinds of things that Jesus actually did and said.[4]

Allegory vs. Symbolism

At this point I must state a very important caveat. Lewis always emphasized that the Narnia stories were not allegories. In fact, Lewis himself only wrote one allegory, *The Pilgrim's Regress*. In a letter to a group of fifth graders in Maryland Lewis wrote that they were mistaken in thinking that everything in the Narnia books represents something in this world. Things do that in Bunyan's *Pilgrim's Progress*, but Lewis insisted he was not writing the Narnia books in that way.[5] Even if *The Chronicles of Narnia* were allegorical, Lewis makes clear elsewhere that an allegory is not the same as a puzzle. The worst thing we can do is to read an allegory with our eyes peeled for clues, like reading a murder mystery.[6]

While the Narnia stories are not allegorical, they do contain symbolism. There is not a one-to-one correspondence between

---

3 Ibid. pp. 47.
4 Lewis, C. S., *Letters to Children*, New York: Macmillan, 1985, p. 52.
5 Ibid. pp. 44-45.
6 See Lewis, C. S., *The Allegory of Love*, New York: Oxford University Press, 1967, p. 333.

everything in Narnia and something in our world, but there are *some* correspondences. There is in the Narnia books what Lewis called a "hidden story".[7] And that hidden story is based upon a supposal. Lewis explains in a letter to a girl named Anne, written on 5 March 1961:

> The whole Narnian story is about Christ. That is to say, I asked myself "Supposing there really were a world like Narnia and supposing it had (like our world) gone wrong, and supposing Christ wanted to go into that world and save it (as He did ours) what might have happened?" The stories are my answer. Since Narnia is a world of Talking Beasts, I thought He would become a Talking Beast there, as he became a Man here. I pictured Him becoming a lion there because (a) The lion is supposed to be the king of beasts: (b) Christ is called "The Lion of Judah" in the Bible: (c) I'd been having strange dreams about lions when I began writing the books. The whole series works out like this:
>
> *The Magician's Nephew* tells the Creation and how evil entered Narnia.
>
> *The Lion etc* – the Crucifixion and Resurrection.
>
> *Prince Caspian* – restoration of the true religion after a corruption.
>
> *The Horse and His Boy* – the calling and conversion of a heathen.
>
> *The Voyage of the Dawn Treader* – the spiritual life (especially in Reepicheep).
>
> *The Silver Chair* – the continued war against the powers of darkness.
>
> *The Last Battle* – the coming of Antichrist (the Ape). The end of the world and the Last Judgement.[8]

---

7   *Letters to Children*, p. 111.
8   Walter Hooper, editor, *The Collected Letters of C. S. Lewis*, Volume III, New York: HarperCollins, 2007, pp. 1244-1245. Lewis' original letter to Anne Waller (now Anne Jenkins) was donated by Anne to Queen's University, Belfast, Northern Ireland. This is very appropriate as Belfast was Lewis' birthplace and Queen's was the university from which Lewis' mother graduated with honors in logic and mathematics. The letter to Anne Waller is part of Queen's Miscellaneous Manuscripts Collection (MS. 1/247) and is on display in their

In a number of Lewis' letters he comments on how children almost always recognize who Aslan is, whereas grown-ups seldom do. However, this book is written for people of all ages who have read the Narnia books and want to understand more of the hidden story behind them all. What I attempt to do in this book is to share with the reader the correspondences I see between Narnia and certain spiritual and biblical themes in our world, as well as demonstrating the connection between what Lewis wrote in the Narnia books and what he wrote elsewhere.

When I first read *The Chronicles of Narnia* I read them in publication order, starting with *The Lion, the Witch and the Wardrobe*. Since that time the books have been re-numbered, following Narnian chronology and the order in which C. S. Lewis himself suggested the books should be read.[9] In this book we will examine each of the Narnia stories following Narnian chronology, starting with *The Magician's Nephew*.

You may wish to use this book to study *The Chronicles* in a group. At the end of each chapter there are discussion questions appropriate for use in a small group, Sunday school class or book discussion group. However you use this book, I hope you enjoy journeying further up and further in to Lewis' classic tales.

C. S. Lewis Reading Room. A facsimile of Lewis' letter to Anne was also incorporated by sculptor Ross Wilson on the back of the wardrobe which is part of his C. S. Lewis Centenary Sculpture outside the Holywood Arches Library in Belfast. Wilson has stated that Lewis' letter to Anne was at least part of the inspiration behind his sculpture.

9 *Letters to Children*, p. 68

Discussion Questions

1. When did you first read, hear or see one of the Narnia stories?
2. If you encountered Narnia as a child, what was that experience like?
3. How is it different reading the Narnia books as an adult? What more do you get out of them?
4. Why do you think the Narnia books have been so popular over the years?
5. When you first read Narnia was the Christian symbolism evident to you? If not, when and how did that symbolism become clear to you?
6. How did you first get interested in reading C. S. Lewis' works? What other Lewis books have you read?
7. What do you hope to get out of this study of Narnia?

I. Creation & Fall
The Magician's Nephew

As Lewis pointed out in his 1961 letter, *The Magician's Nephew* is about the creation of Narnia and how evil entered that fair land. *The Magician's Nephew* is a highly moralistic tale in that it deals extensively with the right way of living (what Lewis called the *Tao*, using a Chinese word). Issues of conscience, good and evil character qualities come up often in this book. We are also here introduced to the chief character behind the *Tao* in all the Narnia stories, the great lion Aslan.

The Magician's Nephew begins with two children from our world, Digory and Polly, entering the Wood between the Worlds, through the use of magic rings created from the dust of Atlantis by Digory's Uncle Andrew. From the Wood between the Worlds, Digory and Polly first get into the world of Charn and meet the terrifying Queen Jadis. Partly by accident, the children end up bringing Jadis back into our world, and then again by accident, they end up taking Jadis, Uncle Andrew, a London cabby and his horse, into the land of Narnia as it is just being created.

Creation

The telling of the creation of Narnia doesn't actually happen until the middle of chapter eight in *The Magician's Nephew*. The first thing that is made clear about the creation of Narnia is that the world of Narnia is created out of nothing or *ex nihilo* as the theologians would say. When Digory, Polly, Uncle Andrew, the Witch, the Cabby and Strawberry the horse first enter Narnia they find themselves standing on something solid, but all is darkness. The Witch remarks about how it is an empty world. The first real thing that happens in the darkness is that a voice begins to sing, a voice which seems to be coming from all around them. As the voice sings on it is suddenly joined by other voices–high, tingly, silvery voices. All at once the sky is filled with a thousand points of light.[10] Digory becomes quite certain it is the stars that are singing, and it is the first voice, the deeper voice, which has created the stars and enabled them to sing. This is all very reminiscent of Job 38:6-7 which talks about the creation of the earth when "the morning stars sang together and all the angels shouted for joy".

It is significant that each of the earthlings and the Witch from Charn respond to the deep voice in different ways. The Cabby is the first one to be intent on listening to the voice; he later remarks that he would have been a better man all his life if he had known there were things like this. (Notice the connection here between the Cabby's experience of the numinous and his own sense of morality. The experience of the numinous can lead one to want to be a better person.[11]) Digory finds the voice so beautiful that it is almost unbearable for him to listen to it. Even the horse responds with a whinny. Uncle Andrew, on the other hand, intensely dislikes the voice and desires to get away from it. The Witch, it appears, understands the song better than anyone else in their group. She recognizes a magic at work which is different and stronger than hers and it fills her with a desire to smash the whole world of Narnia to pieces.

Finally, as the voice swells in the mightiest part of its song the sun arises, and by it the party is able to see all that the voice has created by its singing. At last, they see the singer himself, and upon seeing him they forget everything else, for he is a huge, bright Lion. The Witch immediately wishes to leave the world of Narnia. Uncle Andrew talks about shooting the Lion. The Cabby remarks that the thought of shooting *this* lion is preposterous.

As the Lion continues his song Polly begins to make the connection between the Lion's song and the things popping into existence all

---

10 It is from this phrase, *a thousand points of light*, in *The Magician's Nephew*, a phrase well known to speech writer Peggy Noonan, that U. S. President George H. W. Bush developed the social action theme of his presidency.

11 For more on the connection between the experience of the numinous and morality see Lewis, C. S., *The Problem of Pain*, New York: Macmillan, 1986, pp. 16-21.

around her. Finally, she becomes quite convinced that the Lion is making up all of the things around them out of his own head. Thus Lewis conveys the true understanding of creation *ex nihilo*. When we say that God created the world out of nothing we mean that he created the world out of nothing *other* than himself. He didn't take any pre-existing bits of matter and stick them together to make something else, as we humans do when we create something. No, God made up the world out of things he had in his own mind, just as the Lion created Narnia out of his own head. This truth is expressed in Hebrews 11:3 where it says, "By faith we understand that the universe was formed at God's command, so that what is seen was not made out of what was visible." The only difference in Narnia is that the Lion creates by singing, whereas it would appear that God created our universe by speaking.

A very interesting thing takes place after the Lion creates the first animals in Narnia. The Lion walks among the animals, going up to them two at a time and touching their noses with his. Some animals he passes over, but the ones the Lion chooses immediately step out from among the other animals and follow him. This bit is reminiscent of Noah and the Ark where the animals are chosen two by two to enter the ark and escape the deluge that is about to come on the earth.[12] But in Narnia these animals are not being chosen in order to escape something, rather they are chosen in order to receive a gift. The animals whom the Lion has chosen form a large circle around him, and as the Lion stares intently at them and breathes on them, a flash of fire falls upon the chosen animals, either from the sky or from the Lion himself. This part of the story alludes to the gift of tongues given to the first disciples of Jesus on the day of Pentecost. A violent wind came upon those disciples and tongues of fire came to rest upon them giving them the ability to speak in languages they had not yet learned.[13] In this case the chosen animals of Narnia are made into talking beasts.

The way this event is described in *The Magician's Nephew* correlates with what Lewis has to say in *The Problem of Pain* about the creation of human beings as it relates to evolution. Lewis believed it was

---

12 Genesis 7:2-3.
13 Acts 2:1-4.

possible, and not in conflict with the Bible, to say that God raised one of the primates eventually to become human. Lewis contended that, according to Genesis 2:7, humanity is made out of something else. Man is an animal, but he is an animal called to be or raised to be something more than an animal. Human beings are taken up into a new life without surrendering the old.[14] Lewis theorized that for long centuries God may have perfected the animal form that was to become human and the image of himself. God gave hands to this animal whose thumb could be applied to each of the fingers; God also gave jaws, teeth and throat capable of articulation, and a brain sufficiently complex to execute all the material motions of rational thought.[15]

In the same way, these chosen animals of Narnia are called to be, or raised to be, Talking Beasts, while still remaining animals. It is when the Talking Beasts, along with the Fauns, Satyrs and Dwarfs, first respond to their Creator that we learn the Lion's name – Aslan.[16] The Lion then gives to the creatures themselves, the land of Narnia, the stars and himself. In the same way, God gave to the first man and woman the fish of the sea, the birds of the air, every seed-bearing plant, and the Garden of Eden.[17] Aslan warns the Talking Beasts to beware of going back to the ways of the Dumb Beasts just as God warned Adam not to eat of the tree of the knowledge of good and evil.[18] The idea of the Talking Beasts going back to the ways of the Dumb Beasts echoes Lewis' fear that human beings may some day irreversibly shrink back from true humanity.[19]

Temptation & Fall

The first mention of evil entering Narnia comes in chapter 10 of *The Magician's Nephew*. Aslan tells the Talking Beasts that an evil has

---

14 Lewis, C. S., *Reflections on the Psalms*, San Diego: Harcourt Brace Jovanovich, 1958, p. 115.
15 *The Problem of Pain*, p. 77. See also Lewis' letter to Sister Penelope of January 10, 1952, in *Letters of C. S. Lewis*, p. 417.
16 The name *Aslan* is the Turkish word for lion which C. S. Lewis discovered in Edward William Lane's translation of *The Thousand and One Nights*, better known as *Arabian Nights*. See *Letters to Children*, [22nd January 1952] p. 29.
17 Genesis 1:28-2:16
18 Genesis 2:17.
19 See Lewis, C. S., *The Abolition of Man*, New York: Macmillan, 1978.

already entered Narnia even though that world is only five hours old. The Talking Beasts don't understand what Aslan is talking about–a Neevil or a weevil? As the reader already knows, Aslan is referring to the Witch, Jadis the Queen of Charn. Her entry into Narnia has taken place because Digory earlier gave in to temptation in Charn. The temptation with which Digory was faced in Charn was the temptation to know what would happen if he rang the bell in the center of the hall of images. Note the similarity to the first temptation in our world: the temptation to eat of the tree of knowledge of good and evil.[20] So there is a *fall* which takes place outside Narnia which comes to impact Narnia itself, just as Satan's fall, prior to Eden, came to impact the paradise existence of Eden itself.[21]

However, this is only the prelude to the temptation of Digory *within* Narnia. Because Digory is responsible for bringing evil into Narnia, Aslan charges him with the task of helping to heal Narnia. Aslan commissions Digory to go and get the seed from which a tree will grow in Narnia to protect it from the Witch for years to come. Digory is sent to the center of a garden far away where there grows a very special tree with silver apples. Note that the tree is at the center of a garden just as the tree of life and the tree of the knowledge of good and evil are in the middle of the Garden of Eden.[22] This garden turns out to be a very private place protected by a gate just as Eden and the tree of life are guarded by cherubim and a flaming sword.[23] It is on these gates that Digory reads a verse of warning similar to the verse he read below the bell in Charn; only this verse carries with it no temptation for Digory. One gets the sense that this verse was written by Aslan, whereas the verse in Charn was probably written by the Witch herself.

The difference between Lewis' story and the account in Genesis is that Digory has been instructed to *pick* the apple whereas Adam is

---

20 Genesis 2:17.
21 See Vaus, Will, *Mere Theology*, Downers Grove, Illinois: InterVarsity Press, 2004, pp. 77, 110-111 for more on Lewis' understanding of Satan's fall. See also Genesis 3:1-24, Isaiah 14:12(KJV) and Revelation 12:7-17.
22 Genesis 2:9.
23 See Genesis 3:24. A walled garden is a common picture of Paradise in Persian thought and literature.

instructed *not* to eat of the tree of knowledge of good and evil.[24] Once Digory has plucked one of the silver apples,[25] temptation begins, and it begins *inside* of Digory. As it says in James 1:14, ". . . each one is tempted when, by his own evil desire, he is dragged away and enticed." Digory looks at the apple and smells it before putting it in his pocket; immediately he is filled with a longing to taste the fruit. Next he begins to question the order written on the garden gate. He muses that the command may only have been a suggestion. His mind searches for a loophole that might justify his eating another apple while taking one to Aslan as well. While he is thinking this through he notices a bird in the tree above him, and the bird is watching him. Digory reflects on the idea that you never know who may be watching you in magical places. This suggests the very biblical notion that God's eye is always upon us, his presence is never too far away in the garden.[26]

Digory soon discovers there is another way in which he is not alone; the Witch is with him in the garden. Jadis has violated the warning on the gate and climbed over the wall into the garden. This reminds us of Jesus' statement, "I tell you the truth, the man who does not enter the sheep pen by the gate, but climbs in by some other way, is a thief and a robber."[27] In addition Jadis has eaten one of the apples. Digory runs from her and a chase ensues. Digory stops and threatens to use one of the magic rings and vanish. The Witch tempts him to eat one of the apples by telling him that if he doesn't he will miss some knowledge that would have made him happy his whole life long. This time Digory resists the temptation to knowledge which he had failed

---

24 Genesis 2:17.
25 Golden apples appear in various national mythologies and fairy tales, most notably Greek and Norse mythology with which Lewis was very familiar. Golden apples also figure in Richard Wagner's *Ring* cycle, another Lewis favorite. Silver apples appear in William Butler Yeats' poem *The Song of the Wandering Aengus* of which Lewis would have been aware. Lewis combines the color of Yeats' apples with the meaning behind the golden apples in the Garden of the Hesperides in the rendering of his own myth here in *The Magician's Nephew*. The apples in the Garden of the Hesperides, when eaten, grant to the eater immortality. Notably, Proverbs 25:11 says, "A word aptly spoken is like apples of gold in settings of silver."
26 Genesis 3:8.
27 John 10:1.

to resist in Charn. Next the Witch tempts Digory by telling him that this is the apple of youth which, if he eats it, will make him live forever. Again Digory resists the temptation to eat. But then the Witch uses her best weapon of all, she suggests that Digory could take an apple back to his mother to heal her.[28] This suggestion gives Digory reason to ponder. Having caught Digory in her web of deceit, the Witch continues. She suggests to Digory that Aslan is a wild animal or else something worse. The one thing that seems to save Digory from the Witch's snares is the fact that stealing is unthinkable to him. Digory reminds the Witch and himself of his own promise to Aslan. He remembers that his own mother would not approve of him stealing an apple, even one that would heal her. Digory sees the meanness behind the Witch's suggestion that he should leave Polly behind in order to take the apple secretly to his mother.

Then Digory moves on to the offensive. He asks what the Witch is going to profit from him stealing an apple. It is this offensive move that wins the day, just as the human use of the offensive weapon of the Sword of the Spirit wins the day in battling Satan.[29] And having obeyed Aslan, Digory finds contentment.[30]

The *Tao*

Behind the idea of the fall of Narnia lies the whole concept of ultimate right and wrong, or what Lewis called, the *Tao*. In *The Magician's Nephew* Uncle Andrew's violation of the *Tao* is compared to madness. When Digory brings up the whole issue of right and wrong, Uncle Andrew suggests that the more helpful terms to use would really be broad-minded or narrow-minded. Uncle Andrew and the Witch introduce a blurring of the lines of right and wrong. For instance, is the Witch's throwing of the lamppost bar at Aslan wicked or simply

---

28 Notice that the Witch presents Digory with a series of three temptations, just as Satan presents Jesus with a series of three temptations in the desert (Matthew 4:1-11). And just as Jesus was hungry after forty days of fasting, and therefore tempted to satisfy his hunger by wrong means, so also Digory is hungry from his long journey and tempted to satisfy his hunger by eating one of the silver apples.
29 Ephesians 6:17; Matthew 4:1-11.
30 Lewis, C. S., *The Magician's Nephew*, New York: Macmillan, 1973, p. 166.

spirited? The answer depends upon whom you listen to. Uncle Andrew and the Witch maintain that rules only apply to common people, not to great magicians and queens like themselves. But throughout the story Digory and Polly suggest directly and indirectly that certain actions are decent behavior while other acts are not. For Uncle Andrew, the blowing up of guinea pigs is an appropriate means for him to use to reach the goal of contact with another world. To Digory such an act is simply cruel. The importance of keeping promises is mentioned a few times in the story. Uncle Andrew fails to keep his promise to his godmother and Digory says that breaking one's promise is a rotten thing to do. In contrast, Digory keeps his promise to Aslan to bring him one of the silver apples uneaten.

Why does Digory have such a keen sense of right and wrong? Lewis as narrator suggests it is because commandments such as "Do not steal." were hammered harder into boys' heads more in Digory's time than now. In other words, we have a summary of the *Tao* in the Ten Commandments[31], and if hammered into children's heads it helps to curb bad behavior.[32]

Why then does Uncle Andrew act so wickedly? Answer: because he has seared his own conscience.

Conscience as a guide to the *Tao*

The Apostle Paul says in Romans 2:14-15,

> Indeed, when Gentiles, who do not have the law, do by nature things required by the law, they are a law for themselves, even though they do not have the law, since they show that the requirements of the law are written on their hearts, their consciences also bearing witness, and their thoughts now accusing, now even defending them.

In other words, our conscience serves as a guide to right and wrong, revealing that the *Tao* is written on our hearts.

However, disobedience to conscience can lead to the searing of the conscience.[33] Disobedience to conscience can lead one to the point

---

31 See Exodus 20; Deuteronomy 5.
32 For more about Lewis' views on the *Tao* see *Mere Theology*, pp. 118-121.
33 1 Timothy 4:2

where right and wrong are not recognized anymore. As Lewis points out in *The Magician's Nephew*, what you see and hear depends upon your perspective and character. Uncle Andrew starts out recognizing that the noise in the darkness is a song. But he doesn't like the song, so when the sun rises and he sees the Lion singing, he tries to convince himself that the Lion is not singing but only roaring. As Lewis says, the problem with trying to be dumber than you really are is that you very often succeed. This is what Uncle Andrew did. Eventually he could hear nothing but roaring in the Lion's song. And in the end he couldn't hear anything but roaring even if he wanted to.[34]

Thus Uncle Andrew has made himself unable to hear Aslan's voice. That is what happens when we disobey our conscience, we make ourselves unable to hear God's voice. We come to the place where we have made ourselves so evil that we cannot comprehend goodness, just as the Witch was unable to remember the Wood between the Worlds.[35]

Vices & Virtues

What are the specific virtues and vices, the specific acts of obedience to the *Tao* and deviations from the *Tao*, which Lewis focuses on in *The Magician's Nephew*? There are two major vices we see characterized in this story. The first and foremost is *pride*, what Lewis elsewhere called *the great sin*.[36]

Pride is personified in the characters of Uncle Andrew and Jadis, the Queen of Charn. There is a certain pride of intelligence, or spiritual pride in Uncle Andrew. He considers himself to be a great scholar, a learned magician, to whom ordinary rules do not apply. And yet, as Lewis the narrator points out, Uncle Andrew is like most magicians in that he is working with things he doesn't completely understand. Uncle Andrew's pride is dangerous in that he is willing to sacrifice anything, animals and even humans, in order to achieve his goal of contact with

---

34 *The Magician's Nephew*, p. 171.
35 Ibid. p. 91. For an interesting study of the word *conscience* see C. S. Lewis' *Studies in Words*, Cambridge: Cambridge University Press, 1991, pp. 181-213.
36 See C. S. Lewis, *Mere Christianity*, New York: Macmillan, 1984, pp. 108-114.

another world. But along with this intellectual pride Uncle Andrew also displays a more pardonable form of pride – simple vanity, when he fancies himself as being physically attractive to Jadis. Why is vanity a more pardonable sort of pride? Lewis explains that the vain person wants applause and admiration too much and is always working for it. This is wrong, but it is a child-like or even humble sort of fault. Vanity reveals that you are not completely satisfied with your own admiration alone. You still value other human beings enough to want them to see you. In fact, Lewis says, you're still human, and that's a good sign. The terrible, devilish sort of pride comes in when you look down on other people so much that you don't care anymore what they think.[37]

Jadis is the personification of this more diabolical pride. In Jadis, as in Uncle Andrew, pride and power are associated. As Lewis says in *Mere Christianity* power is what pride really desires. There is nothing that will make a person feel more superior to others than the ability to move them about like pawns. Jadis delights in simply destroying whatever stands in her way, whether they are things or people. Jadis claims it was her sister's pride that destroyed the whole world when in fact it was Jadis' own pride that led her to destroy her sister, and the rest of Charn along with her, by speaking the Deplorable Word.

In contrast to the pride of Uncle Andrew and Jadis we see great humility displayed in the life of Frank the Cabby. While Aslan is creating Narnia with his song the Cabby is the one who tells Uncle Andrew that watching and listening are the things to do, not talking. While this momentous event is taking place Uncle Andrew is completely focused on himself whereas the Cabby is focused on what is going on around him. We see this humility displayed once again when Frank is made the first king of Narnia by Aslan. Frank is astonished at Aslan's suggestion that he should be king; he doesn't think he is fit for the job but he is willing to do whatever Aslan asks of him. Lewis well described the kind of humility embodied in Frank the Cabby when he wrote in *Mere Christianity* that we shouldn't imagine if we meet a really humble person he or she will be what most people call *humble* today. The humble person will not be a sort of sticky marshmallow who is always saying that he or she is nothing. Probably all you will

---
37 Ibid. pp. 112-113.

remember about the humble person is that he or she was cheerful and that he or she took a true interest in what *you* said. You might even feel a bit jealous of anyone who seems to enjoy life so simply. The humble person is not thinking about humility. Humble people don't think of themselves at all.[38]

The second major vice characterized in *The Magician's Nephew* is selfishness. And once again, this vice is personified in Uncle Andrew and Jadis. There is a great possessiveness about Digory's uncle and the Queen. Digory sees through his Uncle's grand words to the core selfishness that is there. Uncle Andrew thinks he can do whatever he wants to gain whatever he desires. The Queen claims it was alright to kill everyone in Charn because they were *her* people. In fact, the Deplorable Word which the Queen speaks is like the atomic bomb.[39] This is the ultimate selfishness: saying in effect: If I can't live then nothing will live.

There is self-centeredness in the Queen's whole way of thinking. She assumes the story is about herself, that the children have been sent from our world to Charn to fetch her. Isn't this the essence of sin, that we assume history is about us as human beings rather than being *His* story, God's story?

The Queen and Uncle Andrew both use people and things rather than appreciating things and people in their separateness, their uniqueness. When Digory is of use to her Jadis pays attention to him but not Polly. When Digory is no longer of use to her she has no regard for him whatsoever and she focuses all of her attention on Uncle Andrew. Similarly, Uncle Andrew wants to *use* the generative properties of Narnia to make money rather than appreciate the beauty of Narnia's fertility.

Digory also desires to use the fruit of Narnia. However, his desire is different; it is for another's good. He wants, if possible and allowable by Aslan, to take the fruit of the tree of life back home to heal his mother. In fact, Digory overcomes his earlier selfishness, his selfish desire for

---

38 Ibid. p. 114.
39 See *The Magician's Nephew*, p. 61. For Lewis' view on the atomic bomb see Lewis, C. S., *Present Concerns*, San Diego: Harcourt Brace Jovanovich, 1986, pp. 73-80.

knowledge, when he surrenders his life to the will of Aslan. Digory, however, does not merely display unselfishness. Rather, he displays the Christian virtue of love.

Lewis distinguishes between the two at the beginning of his sermon, *The Weight of Glory*. Lewis states that if twenty good men were asked in his day what they thought the highest virtue was, nineteen out of twenty would say the highest virtue was unselfishness. However, if any of the great Christians of former times were asked, they would say love was the highest virtue. What has happened is that a positive term has been replaced by a negative one; this is of more than semantic interest. Unselfishness is not mainly about obtaining good things for other people; it is about doing without good things ourselves. Unselfishness makes our own abstinence and not another's happiness the main point. Lewis insists unselfishness is not the same as the Christian virtue of love.[40]

Digory does not merely deprive himself of one of the silver apples, he secures it for Aslan, and eventually, for his mother as well. Digory's act is one of humble love.

One of the virtues Lewis valued most was what might be called a simple homespun goodness. Lewis acquired a love for what he called "homeliness" from his boyhood friend, Arthur Greeves. By homeliness Lewis meant a rooted quality which attaches to all of our simple experiences, to weather, food, the family and the neighborhood. Lewis found this quality in literature such as that of Cowper, Austen, the Brontës, Scott, and the stories of Hans Christian Andersen. He also found it in God's creation.[41]

We see this quality in the character of Aunt Letty, mending a mattress, and again in Frank the Cabby, singing a hymn amidst the darkness before the creation of Narnia. We see this characteristic in the very landscape of Narnia. When Fledge and Digory and Polly make their first stop en route to the Garden of the Silver Apples we read that as they come down nearer to the ground and among the hills the air grows warmer and it is pleasant for them to hear the homely and earthy

---

40 Lewis, C. S., *The Weight of Glory*, New York: Macmillan, 1980, p. 3.
41 See Lewis, C. S., *Surprised by Joy*, New York: Harcourt Brace Jovanovich, 1955, pp. 151-152 and *Letters of C. S. Lewis*, [22 November 1931] p. 294.

sounds again. They listen to the babbling of the brook on its stones and the creaking of trees in the wind. A warm, good smell of sun-baked ground and turf and flowers meets them as they descend.[42] And there is this same quality of homeliness in the simple, good desire of Digory to return to his mother at the end of the story.

Lewis often notes how difficult it is to make good characters attractive in literature. This is true because we know so much more about evil than we do about goodness. Thus most authors find it easier to write about evil characters. To do so one must only write about characteristics of evil one finds in oneself and let them have their head. But for most of us to write about goodness we must begin by traversing a road less traveled. Lewis himself obviously knew something of goodness in his own life because he had the startling ability to make goodness attractive in the characters he wrote about. And Lewis points out the source of such goodness. As he says in *Mere Christianity*, the Christian believes that any good he performs really comes from Christ living in him. A Christian does not believe God will love him because he is good, but that God will make him good because he loves God. In the same way the roof of a greenhouse does not attract the sunlight because of its own brightness. Rather, the roof of the greenhouse becomes bright because the sunbeams shine upon it.[43]

How to handle departures from the *Tao*

But what about the times when we are plainly not good, when we do evil, what do we do then? How are departures from the *Tao* to be handled? And what is evil itself?

Aslan tells us that evil is merely spoiled goodness. Evil is the plucking of good fruit at the wrong time and in the wrong way. Fruit that is taken in this manner is still good, but those who pluck it in the wrong way at the wrong time loathe it ever after.[44]

---

42 *The Magician's Nephew*, p. 149.
43 *Mere Christianity*, p. 63. It is interesting to note that when Lewis wrote this bit about the sun shining on a greenhouse, he may have been looking out the window of his home, The Kilns, at the greenhouse he had in the grounds there.
44 See *Magician's Nephew*, p. 174.

How is evil to be undone? First of all, Lewis makes it evident in *The Magician's Nephew* that there is no escaping the *Tao*, and the consequences of disobedience to the *Tao*. As Digory says to his uncle at the beginning of the book, he never read a story where wicked, cruel magicians, like his uncle, were not paid out in the end. Or as Scripture says, ". . . you may be sure that your sin will find you out."[45]

Second, Lewis says that it is a very sensible thing to think over one's own wicked deeds with the purpose of realizing their wickedness and repenting thereof. Lewis, as narrator, hopes this is what Uncle Andrew will do.[46]

Third, we see Digory confessing his own wrongdoing to Aslan. And Aslan leads him to tell the truth, the whole truth and nothing but the truth. This fleshes out the truth of Proverbs 28:13, "He who conceals his sins does not prosper, but whoever confesses and renounces them finds mercy."

Fourth, Aslan points out the importance of forgiveness in mending broken relationships. He asks Polly if she has forgiven Digory for what he did to her in Charn. She indicates that she has and Aslan says that this is good.

Finally, and most importantly, Aslan promises the Narnians that he will take the worst of evil upon himself. The fulfillment of this promise comes in *The Lion, the Witch and the Wardrobe*.

Aslan: The Person behind the *Tao*

In *Mere Christianity* Lewis talks about a Mind behind the *Tao*, behind the Moral Law. In *The Chronicles of Narnia* Aslan is revealed as the person behind the whole sense of right and wrong that pervades the story. In *The Magician's Nephew* we learn about Aslan through his creation, just as we can learn something about God by looking at the world around us.

What do we learn about Aslan, and at one remove–about God, through reading *The Magician's Nephew*? We learn that Aslan has

---

45 Numbers 32:23.
46 *The Magician's Nephew*, p. 133.

known Frank the Cabby before Frank really knew Aslan.[47] This truth echoes the biblical passages which talk about God foreknowing us[48] and Psalm 139:16 where the psalmist says:

> All the days ordained for me
> were written in your book
> before one of them came to be.

We learn that anyone who hears the call of Aslan will both desire and be able to obey his call.[49] In the same way, those who are called by God are both justified and eventually glorified.[50]

Digory realizes that Aslan is not the sort of person one can bargain with[51] just as Job realizes he spoke too familiarly about God before God spoke to him out of the whirlwind[52] and just as Peter realized that Jesus was not an ordinary man after he saw the miraculous catch of fish.[53]

However, even though Aslan is awe-inspiring he is also one who identifies with Digory's grief.[54] In the same way ". . . we do not have a high priest who is unable to sympathize with our weaknesses . . ."[55]

We serve a God who doesn't need us, and yet he grants us the dignity of playing a part in his salvation plan by carrying his good news to others.[56] In the same way, Aslan doesn't need Digory but he gives Digory the dignity of playing a part in the salvation of Narnia.[57]

In *The Magician's Nephew* we learn about Aslan not only through the eyes of good characters in the story, but also through the eyes of

---

47 Ibid. pp. 163-164.
48 Romans 8:29; I Peter 1:2
49 *The Magician's Nephew*, p. 137.
50 See Romans 8:30.
51 *The Magician's Nephew*, pp. 141-142.
52 See Job 42:1-6.
53 See Luke 5:1-11.
54 *The Magician's Nephew*, p. 142.
55 Hebrews 4:15.
56 See Matthew 28:19-20.
57 See *The Magician's Nephew*, pp. 136, 143. See also Lewis, C. S., *The Four Loves*, San Diego: Harcourt Brace Jovanovich, 1960, pp. 11-12 where Lewis points out that God has no "need-love" of us, for he lacks nothing.

evil ones. It is the Witch who suggests to Digory that Aslan may be a wild animal or something worse.[58] The Witch's suggestion sounds a lot like Lewis' statement in *Mere Christianity* where he says that Jesus either was the Son of God, or else a lunatic or something worse.[59]

And there is one more idea, or manner of thinking, which finds expression in both *The Magician's Nephew* and *Mere Christianity*. In *The Magician's Nephew*, Digory comments about the Wood between the Worlds, about why it is so quiet and sleepy there. He says that nothing ever happens in that wood. In our world it is inside of homes that people have conversations, meals and activities. Nothing happens in the in-between places, between walls, above ceilings, under floors, or in Digory and Polly's attic tunnel. However, Digory says, when one comes out of the attic tunnel one may find oneself in *any* house. So also with the Wood between the Worlds, one might get into any world from there.[60]

In a similar fashion Lewis says that "mere Christianity" is like the entryway to a house, out of which doors open into the various rooms. It is in the rooms, not in the entryway, that there is heat to warm you, furniture on which to rest, and meals to eat. The entryway is a place to wait in, a place from which to check out various rooms, not a place to stay forever.[61]

Thus, the Wood between the Worlds is like mere Christianity, the hall out of which you get to all the other rooms, where you can find meals, warmth and a place to rest. You can get into all the denominations of the one Church from mere Christianity, just as you can get into all the worlds from the Wood between the Worlds.

And just as mere Christianity serves as an introduction to the Church, so *The Magician's Nephew* serves as our introduction to all the other Narnia books and, most importantly, to Aslan himself, the memory of whom makes all things well.[62]

---

58 See *The Magician's Nephew*, p. 162.
59 *Mere Christianity*, p. 56.
60 *The Magician's Nephew*, p. 35.
61 *Mere Christianity*, p. 12.
62 *The Magician's Nephew*, p. 179. This line from *The Magician's Nephew* is reminiscent of one of the statements of an author Lewis enjoyed, Lady Julian

Discussion Questions

1. What do you think of the moral themes in *The Magician's Nephew*?
2. Does Lewis make the supernatural realm believable in this story? If so, how?
3. After reading this book, what would you guess was Lewis' view of magic? Why?
4. What does this book teach us about Lewis' view of kingship?
5. How do you respond to the account of the creation of Narnia? Does it capture your imagination more or less than the biblical account of creation? Why?
6. What did you feel as you read about Jadis tempting Digory in the Garden? What does this story teach us about how to handle temptation?
7. How might we assess each character in this story according to their reaction to Aslan?

---

of Norwich, who once said, "All shall be well, and all shall be well, and all manner of things shall be well." See *Letters of C. S. Lewis*, [2 June 1940] p. 352. Original source: Julian of Norwich, *Revelations of Divine Love*, London: Penguin, 1998, p. 80

II. CRUCIFIXION & RESURRECTION
The Lion, the Witch and the Wardrobe

According to C. S. Lewis, the major spiritual theme of *The Lion, the Witch and the Wardrobe* is that of the Crucifixion and the Resurrection. But before we get to the central spiritual theme of this book we discover some other important themes as well.

The Experience of the Numinous

The first thing that envelops the reader of *The Lion, the Witch and the Wardrobe* is the atmosphere. From the moment the four Pevensie children enter the professor's house there is adventure afoot, and a certain air of mystery. The intrigue grows as first Lucy then the rest of the children discover the magical wardrobe and the doorway to Narnia. The experience of traveling to Narnia creates a longing in Lucy to go there again. It is a longing deepened by the fact that she can't seem to get back into Narnia whenever she wants. Sometimes the wardrobe leads to fir trees and snow crunching underfoot, other times it contains only mothballs and fur coats with a solid wood back.

The experience of what the Germans call *Sehnsucht* and Lewis came to call Joy grows in the children once they all enter Narnia together. When Mr. Beaver mentions the name of Aslan each of the children feel something jump inside. Edmund feels a mysterious sense of horror. Peter feels suddenly brave and adventurous. Susan feels as though a delicious smell or a delightful strain of music has just floated by her. Lucy feels like one does upon waking on the morning of the first day of summer vacation.

Lewis talks about a similar experience in a number of his works. In his autobiography he calls it Joy. In *The Pilgrim's Regress* he calls it romanticism. In his sermon, *The Weight of Glory*, he calls it an inconsolable longing. And in *The Problem of Pain* he talks about the experience of the numinous. When speaking of this experience in *The Problem of Pain* Lewis says that the numinous is either a quirk of the human mind, albeit a quirk shared by the most developed poets, philosophers and saints, or else the numinous is an immediate experience of something truly supernatural, to which the title *revelation* should really be given.[63]

Lewis notes that this experience of the numinous is a common strand in all developed religion. A second common strand in all religion is morality. This too we see in *The Lion, the Witch and the Wardrobe*.

Right & Wrong

We encounter a sense of morality in *The Lion* just as we do in *The Magician's Nephew*. We first come across it when Lucy meets Mr. Tumnus. The Faun weeps contritely when he realizes what a horrible thing he had planned to do in kidnapping Lucy. Tumnus realizes inside himself, once he has gotten to know the human child, he cannot hand her over to the White Witch. There is obviously a sense of conscience within characters in the world of Narnia, just as there is a sense of conscience in us as human beings. And so the Faun escorts Lucy safely back to the lamp-post.

The theme of right and wrong continues when Edmund gives in to the temptation of the White Witch (more on that in a moment). Edmund realizes it is going to be no fun for him once he and Lucy return to the professor's house because he will have to admit that Lucy was right all along. Betrayal of his own conscience even leads to sickness in Edmund's stomach.[64] And then, Lewis as narrator tells us, Edmund decides to do the nastiest thing possible, he decides to let Lucy down. Edmund tells Peter and Susan that he and Lucy were only pretending about Narnia.

The theme of obedience to conscience appears again once all four children enter Narnia together. Upon finding Mr. Tumnus' cave

---

63 *The Problem of Pain*, pp. 20-21.
64 Edmund is conscience-stricken just as King David was on at least a couple of occasions. See 1 Samuel 24:5 and 2 Samuel 24:10.

ransacked, Peter, Susan and Lucy all realize they must do something to help free the faun from the clutches of the White Witch. The children have a sense of duty which overrides their natural instincts of self-preservation.

In *Mere Christianity* Lewis shows how our human sense of morality is not merely an instinct. He states that if two instincts are in competition, and there is nothing in a person's brain except these two instincts, of course the stronger instinct will win. However, when we are most aware of a sense of moral law, that law usually tells us to obey the weaker instinct. Everyone wants to preserve their own life more than they really want to help a drowning person, but the moral law, or the *Tao*, tells us to help the drowning person anyway. [65] Clearly there is something more than instinct in operation in the human psyche. There is a real law operating, over and above all our instincts, telling us what we *should* do.

This point from *Mere Christianity* is perfectly illustrated in the children's battle with conscience at Mr. Tumnus' cave. The children, in one sense, don't really want to get involved in fighting a witch in a strange and dangerous new world. They are afraid of what such action might cost them. But it doesn't seem right *not* to help Mr. Tumnus. It is because of Lucy that the faun is in trouble. So the Pevensies conclude that they simply *must* help the faun if there is any way for them to do so.

What is it that convinces the Pevensies they *must* help Mr. Tumnus? It is nothing other than conscience. Their conscience, their mental awareness of the moral law, tells them to help the faun. And I imagine that they, at least Peter, Susan and Lucy, do not want to have the sick feeling in their stomach Edmund had earlier. They want to have clear consciences.[66] So, in the end they choose to do what is right.

---

65 *Mere Christianity*, pp. 22-23.
66 The importance of keeping a clear conscience is mentioned throughout the Bible. See Genesis 20:5-6; 1 Samuel 25:31; Job 27:6; Acts 23:1; 24:16; Romans 9:1; 13:5; 1 Corinthians 4:4; 2 Corinthians 1:12; 1 Timothy 1:19; 3:9; 2 Timothy 1:3; Hebrews 9:9; 10:22; 13:18; 1 Peter 3:16,21.

Temptation

The theme of temptation appears throughout *The Chronicles of Narnia*. However, the first encounter between Edmund and the White Witch is perhaps the most memorable temptation scene of all.

It is important to remember that when we are first introduced to the White Witch we are not told, explicitly, that she is a witch at all. Rather we are told that she is a great lady, taller than any woman Edmund had met before, and she is beautiful. There is something attractive about the White Witch; otherwise, Edmund might have run from her immediately.

In the same way, there is something attractive about evil; otherwise we might never do wrong. As Lewis says elsewhere, evil is only spoiled goodness. The only way evil can exist is by corrupting what is good; after all, existence itself is a good. Evil would not be tempting unless it were for the good still in it. Satan himself is a fallen angel and even appears as an angel of light.[67] The devil is a corruption of something good in God's creation. Temptation happens when we are enticed by our own desires.[68] These longings are, perhaps, for good things. However, they are longings which have been corrupted and which now lead us to take good things for ourselves, at the wrong time, in the wrong way, for the wrong, selfish reasons.

The Queen tempts Edmund with something good that he enjoys eating – Turkish Delight.[69] The difference with this Turkish Delight is that it is magical; it has an addictive quality that makes the consumer want more and more of it. In fact, the person eating this Turkish Delight would eat his fill unto death if he could.

In this brief passage Lewis captures the addictive nature of certain temptations; one thinks of smoking, drinking alcohol, taking certain drugs, eating, sex, just to name a few things that, like Turkish Delight, may not be bad in and of themselves, but can become addictive behaviors

---

67 2 Corinthians 11:14
68 See James 1:14.
69 *Turkish Delight* (or Lokum) is the name of a gelatin sort of candy produced in Turkey since the 15th century and introduced in England and other Western countries in the 19th century. It is often covered with chocolate to make it more interesting. My children and I have often enjoyed the non-magical variety.

for certain people, if not all people. In fact, there is something in our sinful nature, as human beings, which causes us to never be content with a moderate amount of a pleasure. Rather, we are often tempted to pray that fatal prayer – "Encore!"[70] We strive for, or even ask God to give us, more of the same pleasure over again, rather than being satisfied with what God has already given us and moving on to new pleasures.

Such was the case with Edmund and the Turkish Delight. It would seem there was an emptiness in Edmund's life that he was trying to fill. Perhaps Edmund was the proverbial middle child among his three siblings. Perhaps he felt unnoticed or left out. Maybe he felt that Lucy, as the youngest in the family, got all the attention. At any rate, he couldn't stand it any more. Upon meeting the White Witch Edmund finds something, or someone, whom he thinks, unconsciously, might fill his inner emptiness. The Queen promises him recognition and even power over his siblings as the new Prince, and eventually King of Narnia. This promise, along with Edmund's craving for the Turkish Delight, makes him willing to sacrifice his own family members, in order to have his own emptiness filled.

In reality the White Witch is offering Edmund something which is not hers to give. She is not the rightful heir to the throne of Narnia and so it is not her prerogative to pass that authority on to another. What the White Witch offers by theft, Aslan is not only willing, but wanting to give to Edmund by divine right.

It all sounds vaguely familiar, doesn't it? It sounds just like the serpent in the Garden of Eden who offers to make Adam and Eve like God once they have tasted of the fruit of the tree of knowledge of good and evil. Adam and Eve don't even pause to think that they have already been created in God's image. The serpent is offering them something which is not his to impart and which, in fact, is already theirs. It is the same story of temptation with Edmund and the White Witch.

---

70 Lewis talks about this in *Letters to Malcolm: Chiefly on Prayer*, New York: Harcourt, Brace, Jovanovich, 1964, p. 27.

Logic

If Edmund only thought through the whole situation logically he might eventually have abandoned his hope of the White Witch supplying him with anything he really needed. If he had only waited to find out that Aslan, as Son of the Emperor-beyond-the-Sea, wanted to make him a rightful King of Narnia, perhaps Edmund could have turned from his evil path earlier.

Logic, as much as longing, can lead a person to the truth. These twin guides led Lewis himself back to the truth of the Christian faith. That's why the subtitle to *The Pilgrim's Regress*, Lewis' allegorical account of his own conversion, was: *An Allegorical Apology for Christianity, Reason and Romanticism*, reason being another word for logic, and romanticism being another word for longing.

Logic is very important in *The Lion, the Witch and the Wardrobe*. Thus the professor questions why the Pevensies aren't taught logic at school. The professor proceeds to introduce Peter and Susan to a very familiar sounding logical trilemma. The children have approached the professor in fear that Lucy may be going mad since she insists that Narnia is real. In response, the professor shows Peter and Susan that there are only three alternatives. Either Lucy is a liar, or she is a lunatic, or she is telling the truth. Peter and Susan have not known Lucy to lie in the past. And the professor says Lucy is obviously not crazy. So then, the professor maintains, the only logical conclusion is that Lucy is telling the truth.[71]

The logic which the professor presents in this passage in *The Lion, the Witch and the Wardrobe* is very similar to the logic Lewis presents in *Mere Christianity*. In the latter book Lewis states that either Jesus was, and is, the Son of God, or else he was crazy, or perhaps something worse. We may dismiss Jesus as a fool, we can denounce him as a demon, or we can bow before him and call him divine. But we simply cannot persist with the nonsense of calling him a great human teacher. Jesus himself hasn't left that option open to us.[72]

---

71 Lewis, C. S., *The Lion, the Witch and the Wardrobe*, New York: Macmillan, 1970, p. 45.
72 *Mere Christianity*, p. 56.

So even in telling the story of *The Lion, the Witch and the Wardrobe* Lewis is obviously trying to get us, his readers, to think logically and he is preparing us for the kind of logic he presents in *Mere Christianity*.

The Person of Aslan

The great lion Aslan is Lewis' picture of what Christ would look like in a land of Talking Beasts. Aslan is Lewis' answer to the question: If God needed to save a land of talking animals, how would he do it in such a world? In Aslan Lewis manages to mirror the nature and character of Christ. Aslan is the Son of the Emperor-beyond-the-Sea, thus suggesting the first two persons of the Trinity—Father and Son. There is a terrifying goodness about Aslan, a severe tenderness about him, which is very much like the character of the Jesus whom we see in the Gospels. Aslan is not a tame lion; he isn't safe, but he is good. The awesome nature of Aslan makes it difficult for the children to even look at him when they first meet him.

Encounters with Aslan

Throughout *The Lion, the Witch and the Wardrobe* we see the importance of personal encounters with Aslan. When Peter, Susan and Lucy first meet Aslan, Peter is quick to accept blame for Edmund going wrong. There is something about being in Aslan's presence, a holiness about him, which makes Peter more keenly aware of his own wrongdoing, just as Isaiah became aware that he was a man of unclean lips as he encountered the holiness of the Lord in his throne room.[73] Aslan does nothing to either excuse or blame Peter; he simply looks at Peter with his deep, golden eyes.[74]

Lucy, upon encountering Aslan, immediately asks if anything can be done to save Edmund. She and her siblings have been told by Mr. Beaver that it is Aslan alone who can save Mr. Tumnus.[75] Also according to Mr. Beaver, Aslan is their only chance of rescuing Edmund.[76] So it is quite natural for Lucy to look to Aslan as a savior. Aslan tells her that

---

73 See Isaiah 6:1-5.
74 *The Lion, the Witch and the Wardrobe*, p. 124.
75 Ibid. p. 74.
76 Ibid. p. 82.

all shall be done to rescue her brother, but that it may be more difficult than she thinks.

After this Aslan takes Peter off, alone, to view the castle of Cair Paravel in the distance, laying his heavy paw upon Peter's shoulder as they walk together. Aslan explains to Peter that he is to be the High King and sit in one of the four thrones at Cair. Later, Peter and Aslan walk together to the Fords of Beruna, discussing the battle plan for fighting the witch, along the way. Peter asks Aslan if he will be there for the battle, but Aslan gives him no such assurance.

We are not told much of anything about Edmund's first encounter with Aslan. The two walk together in the dewy grass after Edmund's rescue and we are told a conversation took place which Edmund never forgot.[77] Aslan tells Edmund's siblings they need not talk to him about the past, and Edmund tells them he is sorry for his rotten behavior. Whatever took place in Aslan's conversation with Edmund it helped the boy to get over thinking about himself and it focused his attention on Aslan, even later when the White Witch was accusing him.[78] Something about Aslan's conversation with Edmund causes the boy to trust in the Lion and wait for him to work things out with the witch.[79]

One of the most moving encounters with Aslan in this story is when Lucy and Susan find Aslan, late at night, walking slowly back up the hill to the Stone Table. Aslan welcomes their company and comfort in his loneliness. At Aslan's invitation the girls bury their cold hands in his fur. But the girls can only accompany Aslan just so far. He has them stop and hide themselves a safe distance away from the Stone Table itself.

In each of these personal encounters with Aslan we are reminded of something important about spending time alone, spiritually, with Christ. When we meet Christ in the secret place there will be an awareness of his holiness and our sinfulness, adoration followed by confession. When we meet with Christ our next greatest concern should be the salvation of our friends and family. This too we should bring

---

77 Ibid., p. 135.
78 Ibid. p. 138.
79 Ibid. p. 140.

before him in prayer, trusting that he will do all in his power to rescue those we pray for. Lewis also teaches us through these encounters that prayer can be a sort of two-way communication. We need to let Christ communicate his plans to us just as Aslan communicated to Peter. Edmund's meeting with Aslan teaches us the importance of being enraptured with Christ and keeping our focus on him at all times, especially when evil is close-by. Susan and Lucy's night journey with Aslan reminds us that perhaps we can bring encouragement to the heart of God, when we walk with him and talk with him.

The Work of Aslan

Lewis pictures the work of Christ as well as the character of Christ in the activities of Aslan. Aslan is the Savior of Edmund, Tumnus and all Narnia; in fact, we are told that Aslan is the only one who can fulfill the function of Savior. Aslan is most especially a Savior in that he gives his life for Edmund as a substitute. Aslan describes his own sacrifice as that of a willing victim who had committed no treachery but who was killed in a traitor's stead. When such a victim offers himself as a substitute, death itself starts working backwards.[80]

In Aslan's death on the Stone Table Lewis pictures for us what he believed to be the central truth of Christianity. In *Mere Christianity* Lewis says that the center of Christianity has to do with Christ's death. By that death Jesus has somehow put us right with God and given us a new start. Theories as to how his death accomplished this are less important than the fact of the saving death itself.[81]

Lewis explains the efficacy of Aslan's death in magical terms, thus suggesting that *how* it works is really beyond our human comprehension. The important thing is for Edmund to trust in what Aslan does for him. The vital thing for us is to trust in what Christ has done for us. Edmund benefits from Aslan's death without fully understanding it. So too, we can benefit from Christ's death without fully understanding it, just as a person can benefit from eating good food, whether or not he or she understands certain theories about vitamins.

---

80 Ibid., pp. 159-160.
81 *Mere Christianity*, p. 57.

The resurrection of Aslan is a physical one, for Lewis believed in Christ's physical resurrection.[82] The resurrection is tied to the death as a vindication of the one who was a willing and innocent victim. Susan and Lucy are afraid at first that the risen Aslan might be a ghost[83] just as the disciples were afraid that the risen Jesus might be a phantom.[84] Aslan licks Susan's forehead to assure her he is not a ghost. So too Jesus invites his disciples to touch him and he eats a piece of broiled fish in their presence to assure them he has been raised bodily to new life.

Aslan as Sovereign

Aslan is clearly the sovereign Lord of Narnia. We see Aslan's sovereign love in that he *initiates* Edmund's salvation. Edmund doesn't seek out Aslan to free him from the control of the White Witch. At first, Edmund is running away from Aslan, just as all of us tend to run away from God in our self-centeredness.[85] Edmund is the Judas of this story, betraying Aslan, and even his own brother and sisters, to the White Witch.[86] Once Edmund realizes how evil the White Witch is, as soon as he would like to run away from her, he is entrapped. Edmund can't rescue himself. He needs a Rescuer. And that is exactly what Aslan becomes for Edmund.

Aslan as Giver of New Life

One of many dramatic incidents from *The Lion, The Witch and The Wardrobe* takes place after Aslan's resurrection. Susan and Lucy accompany Aslan to the castle of the White Witch. At the castle, Aslan breathes on all of the creatures whom the White Witch has turned to stone, and they come to life again. This gives us a very dramatic portrait of what the Bible calls regeneration, or the new birth. In Ezekiel 36:26 the Lord says, "I will give you a new heart and put a new spirit in you; I will remove from you your heart of stone and give you a heart of flesh." Aslan breathing on the stone figures is also reminiscent of the Lord

---

82 See Lewis, C. S., *Miracles*, New York: Macmillan, 1978, pp. 143-148.
83 *The Lion, the Witch and the Wardrobe*, p. 159.
84 See Luke 24:36-43.
85 See Romans 3:10-11.
86 However, unlike Judas in the Gospels, Edmund is saved in the end.

breathing on the disciples in the Upper Room,[87] though the former was for the purpose of regeneration, as it were, whereas the latter was for the purpose of mission.[88] So in Aslan breathing on the stone figures we get a picture of the work of Christ, but also the work of the Holy Spirit.

The Identity of Aslan

According to a letter that Lewis wrote to one of his child readers, he placed Father Christmas in the story specifically to identify Aslan as the Christ figure, someone who "arrived" at the same time as Father Christmas.[89] Douglas Gresham, Lewis' step-son, suggests that this was the reason why Lewis retained the character of Father Christmas in the story of *The Lion, the Witch and the Wardrobe*, even after friends like Tolkien told him that they felt Father Christmas was out of place. According to Gresham, Father Christmas, in his giving of gifts to the children and to the beavers, is symbolic of the Holy Spirit as the giver of spiritual gifts, and Lewis felt it was important to maintain that aspect of the story.[90]

Aslan arrives in Narnia during the winter, at the same time as Father Christmas, and Aslan's passion takes place in the spring, dovetailing with the life of Christ and the church calendar in our world. As in the Gospel accounts so it is in the story of Aslan that women are the last of his followers with him at his death, and the first to witness his resurrection. After his resurrection it is Aslan who kills the White Witch just as the book of Revelation tells us that Jesus will one day utterly defeat Satan.

Aslan, the Humble King

Aslan also reflects to us the humble kingship of Jesus. There is a lovely line in *The Lion, the Witch and the Wardrobe* where the great lion Aslan is leading all the talking beasts off to war with the White Witch. He says to the animals that those who have a keen sense of smell must

---

[87] John 20:22.
[88] For this insight I am indebted to Kilby, Clyde S., *Images of Salvation*, Harold Shaw Publishers, Wheaton, 1978, p. 63.
[89] *Letters to Children*, [June 3rd 1953] p. 32.
[90] Lecture on *The Chronicles of Narnia* delivered by Douglas Gresham at Murrysville Community Church, Murrysville, Pennsylvania in October 1998.

come in front with *us lions* to sniff out where the battle is taking place. The other lion immediately picks up on Aslan's words and is thrilled at Aslan saying: *us lions!* The other lion loves the fact that there is no standoffishness with Aslan.[91]

In a similar way Jesus was a humble king like Aslan. He rode on a donkey into Jerusalem, not on a war-like charger. Jesus shared ministry with his disciples. And Jesus said that "the Son of Man did not come to be served, but to serve, and to give his life as a ransom for many."[92]

A Wild Romp

While Lewis shows us much that Aslan and Christ share in common he also adds his own unique touches to this story of rescue. One of those unique contributions is the scene where Susan and Lucy ride on Aslan's back after he comes back to life. What could be a more dynamic picture of the believer's relationship with the living Christ? Rather than simply walking with him, we are called to ride on his back. He is the driver and conveyer of the believer in this wild romp called the Christian life.

The great thing about Lewis is that he sees life in epic proportions and he helps his readers to do the same. Not only are we called to untamed travel on Aslan's back, but we, like the Pevensie children, are called to reign with Aslan.[93] What could be more exciting than that?

In *The Lion, the Witch and the Wardrobe* Lewis gives us a foretaste of a life we have only dreamed of. He gives us, who live in the frosts and east winds of Old Nature, the fragrance of spring flowers, the aroma of a New Nature to enjoy.[94] Lewis' story is only a picture, but it is a picture, like the picture of the *Dawn Treader* in Eustace's house, that we are invited to step into. And if we accept that invitation, there will be even greater realms to explore, further up and further in.

---

91 *The Lion, the Witch and the Wardrobe*, pp. 171-172.
92 Mark 10:45.
93 Ephesians 2:6.
94 I am paraphrasing what Lewis says in *Miracles* at the end of the chapter on "Miracles of the Old Creation".

Discussion Questions

1. When the Pevensie children first hear the name of Aslan, each has a different reaction. Does this story fill you with a sense of longing, as the name of Aslan did for three of the children? Or have you ever had an experience of the numinous as Lewis describes in this story? Explain.

2. What do you think of Lewis' portrayal of evil in the character of the White Witch? The White Witch tempted Edmund with food. What temptation works best on you?

3. Do you find Lewis' portrayal of Aslan as a lion who is not safe, but good, an attractive one? Would you like to get to know Aslan? Why or why not?

4. When Aslan comes on the scene he puts all to right, as Mr. Beaver says. What do you think of Lewis' holistic view of salvation, encompassing all of creation?

5. The climactic event of this story is the killing of Aslan by the White Witch and his coming to life again. How does this part of the story make you feel? How would you have felt if you were Edmund?

6. Do you think the Christian life is like a ride on Aslan's back? How do you respond to this image?

7. Lewis obviously believed in myth as an excellent means of communicating truth. What do you think of this? Do you prefer reading a story, or a book with principles and "how to" explanations?

III. Calling & Conversion
The Horse and His Boy

All of Lewis' Narnia tales fill the sensitive reader with a sense of longing. It was the experience of longing, what the Germans call *Sehnsucht*, and Lewis called joy, that led Lewis himself to personal faith in Jesus Christ.

For Lewis, this sense of longing was often stirred through literature. One particular piece of literature which awakened a sense of *Sehnsucht* in Lewis' youth was *Tegner's Drapa*.[95] Upon reading about Balder, Lewis says he was instantly lifted up into a vast expanse of northern sky. He desired with a frightful intensity something which he could not fully describe except to say that it was cold, spacious, severe, pale, and remote. At the very moment of experiencing this longing he found himself already falling out of the desire and wishing he was back in it.[96]

This longing for "Northernness" came back to the young Lewis when he was a student at Cherbourg school in Great Malvern, England in his early teens. He came across an advertisement for the book, *Siegfried and the Twilight of the Gods* illustrated by Arthur Rackham. Lewis later wrote that at that moment pure "Northernness" engulfed him. He had a vision of large, open spaces hanging above the Atlantic Ocean in an endless twilight of northern summer. As Lewis was having this reaction to Arthur Rackham's picture he realized he had met this same feeling before, in *Tegner's Drapa*. He recognized that Siegfried belonged to the same world as Balder and the sunward-sailing cranes. With the plunge back into his own past there arose at once in his mind

---

95 A Norse ballad by Henry Wadsworth Longfellow, written in 1847.
96 *Surprised by Joy*, p. 17.

the memory of joy itself. He realized he was having, once again, the same experience he had lacked for years; he felt like he was returning from exile to his own country.[97]

Lewis' love of Northernness led to a love of Wagnerian music: *The Ride of the Valkyries*, the *Ring*, *Lohengrin* and *Parsifal*. The hunger for Northernness eventually led Lewis to write his own tragedy, Norse in subject and Greek in form, entitled *Loki Bound*. A shared longing for the North is also what initially drew Lewis' heart to his life-long friend Arthur Greeves. The first time Lewis had a serious conversation with Greeves the latter was sitting in bed and on a table beside him lay a copy of *Myths of the Norsemen*. Lewis quickly discovered that both of them had known the attack of *Sehnsucht* and that, for both, the attack was launched from the North.[98]

Narnia and the North

What does all of this have to do with *The Horse and His Boy*? Interestingly enough, one of the titles Lewis suggested for the book, before the publisher settled on the present title, was: *Narnia and the North*.

Shasta has a longing for the north just like Lewis. When Shasta is sitting out of doors mending nets he often looks eagerly to the north. Beyond the hill, which is the horizon of his world, Shasta dreams that there must be some delightful secret his father wishes to hide from him. In fact, Shasta himself has blond hair, and comes to realize that he is from the north. The constant refrain throughout the book is "Narnia and the North". It is the constant direction toward which the action of the book leads. When Shasta sees the Narnians for the first time, some of them are wearing helmets with wings like the Valkyries.[99] It is, in part, a longing for the North that draws Shasta, Bree, Aravis and Hwin on to their journey together.

---

97 Ibid. p. 73. Lewis came to love Proverbs 25:25 (KJV) which is quoted on the title page of *The Pilgrim's Regress*: "As cold waters to a thirsty soul, so is good news from a far country."
98 Ibid. p. 130.
99 Lewis, C. S., *The Horse and His Boy*, New York: Macmillan, 1980, p. 55.

The Journey

The theme of "the journey" is a powerful one in *The Horse and His Boy*. In this story all four main characters – Shasta, Bree, Aravis and Hwin journey from slavery to freedom.

Amazingly enough, Shasta's introduction to slavery comes from Aslan and is for the purpose of protection, for it is Aslan who guides the boat in which Shasta lies, a baby near death, to the place where Arsheesh, the fisherman, receives him. This corresponds to the biblical theme of Israel's slavery in Egypt. Jacob and his family initially go down to Egypt to escape famine; they are cared for in a foreign territory by the skillful hands of Joseph, providing for his family. But eventually a Pharaoh arises who knows not Joseph. So what begins as a means of God's protection and provision for Israel turns into cruel enslavement. So it is with Shasta.

Another biblical theme is also interwoven into this story. Just as Shasta is really the son of a king but does not know his true identity, so too, from a biblical perspective, we are all sons and daughters of the king. However, we are sons and daughters who have become slaves, forgotten our true identity, and therefore are in need of rescue. The fact that Shasta is a prince of Archenland without knowing it suggests that in our world there may be some who are outside of Christendom but who belong to Christ without knowing it.

What effect does slavery have on Shasta's life? Shasta is, of course, impoverished, symbolized in the story by the fact that he has no shoes.[100] But what slavery does to the inner man is far more devastating than what it does to the outer man. The slave experience breeds in Shasta lack of trust.[101] He thinks of himself as a "nobody".[102]

The turning point on the journey from slavery to freedom happens for Shasta while he is in Tashbaan. It is in Tashbaan that Shasta begins to suspect his real identity, after spending time with the Narnians.[103] The movement from slavery to freedom not only involves for Shasta a

---

100 Ibid. p. 125.
101 Ibid. p. 70.
102 Ibid. p. 74.
103 Ibid. p. 76.

dawning recognition of his real identity but also a turning away from his old way of life. Shasta begins to change when he is at the tombs. For one thing, after experiencing the cat's protection among the eerie tombs Shasta promises never to treat a cat badly again![104]

The character of Aravis gives us a female perspective on the journey from slavery to freedom. Aravis's slavery is different from Shasta's for her slavery consists in being a woman in a society which doesn't properly respect women. Aravis looks forward to going to a land where no woman is forced to marry against her will.[105] Aravis, like Shasta, begins to change after her time in Tashbaan. For Aravis the thing which changes her is her reunion with her silly young friend Lasaraleen.[106] Aravis even begins to like simple Narnian fashions better than the overdone Calormene counterparts.[107]

In the end, Aravis's journey from slavery to freedom requires that she be severely scratched by Aslan's claws.[108] Aslan explains that the scratches on her back are, tear for tear, throb for throb, blood for blood, equal to the stripes laid on the back of Aravis's stepmother's slave because of the drugged sleep Aravis cast upon her. Aslan tells Aravis that she needed to know what it felt like. In fact, this experience causes Aravis to start caring for someone other than herself. She asks Aslan if any more harm will come to the slave because of her actions. But Aslan refuses to answer Aravis's question for – as he says more than once in the story – he tells no one any story but their own. Aslan's attack also causes Aravis to see how wrongly she has treated Shasta during their journey and how brave Shasta really is.

Like the humans, the horses, Bree and Hwin, are also on a journey from slavery to freedom. Along their journey they must learn that freedom requires discipline. They must learn to push themselves as hard as they were once pushed by their human masters.[109]

---

104 Ibid. p. 86.
105 Ibid. p. 36.
106 Ibid. p. 99.
107 Ibid. p. 104.
108 Ibid. p. 194.
109 Ibid. pp. 131, 136.

For Bree more than for Hwin, there are inner hang-ups from which he needs to be freed–mainly his pride. A combination of pride, and its counterpart – self-loathing, cause Bree to think he is not fit for freedom.[110] Bree condemns himself for not being brave enough to rescue Aravis and Hwin when they are being attacked by Aslan.

Throughout the story, Bree is the one who has been most aggressively pursuing freedom. He is the one who encourages Shasta to run away with him. He is constantly talking about Narnia and the North and what it will be like to live as a free horse in Narnia again. But in the end, Bree discovers that freedom is not something to be grasped rather it must be received as a gift from Aslan. And when Bree finally comes close to tasting freedom back in Narnia, he is afraid of it. He is afraid there will be no more rolls in the grass.[111] In a similar way, we humans sometimes think that serving God will be terrible, when in reality it is the greatest joy.

Hwin is the one character in the story in which transformation from inner slavery to freedom happens almost instantaneously. Hwin, apparently, has the least inner problems to overcome. When she meets Aslan she immediately tells him how beautiful he is, and that he may eat her if he likes. She says that she would sooner be eaten by Aslan than fed by anyone else. Aslan then plants a lion's kiss on her twitching, velvet nose and tells her that he knew she would not be long in coming to him. He promises Hwin that joy shall be hers.[112]

Values

Along the journey with Shasta, Bree, Aravis and Hwin, we subtly learn some lessons, not only about slavery and freedom, but about values in general.

We learn lessons about honor and treachery. Rabadash is the treacherous one, attacking Archenland unprovoked, for completely selfish reasons. But in contrast, King Lune shows great restraint and honor by not having Rabadash executed once he is caught.[113]

---

110 Ibid. p. 145.
111 Ibid. p. 202.
112 Ibid. p. 193.
113 Ibid. p. 187.

The issue of stealing comes up throughout the story. On the morning after their escape, Shasta asks Bree if using the Tarkaan's money will be stealing. Bree says he never thought of it that way. Bree suggests that since he and Shasta are prisoners in enemy territory, using the money will be like using booty, the spoils of war.[114] Shasta gives in to this rationale throughout the story, but overall, his conscience is more sensitive than Bree's.[115]

Shasta is always concerned about doing what is right. When Aravis tells the story of drugging her stepmother's servant, Shasta is concerned about what happened to the servant.[116] However, Shasta is not perfect in his goodness. He is not very respectful of Aravis, at first. He often acts out of a sense of inferiority, a reverse sort of pride. When he is "kidnapped" by the Narnians he hopes that the real Corin will not show up, so that he, Shasta, can be whisked off to Narnia by boat rather than having to make the arduous journey across the desert. Shasta is not concerned, at that moment, with the fate of the real Corin. Nor is he very concerned with what will happen to Bree, Hwin and Aravis if he does not show up at the tombs.[117] When the real Corin does show up Shasta at first suggests that Corin not tell the other Narnians about their switching places, until he realizes that this lie will be immediately betrayed by Corin's bruises. Shasta's natural bent to dissembling is contrasted to Corin's honesty.[118] Shasta's self-centeredness turns to self-pity when he is alone on the mountain, after meeting up with King Lune and the party of Archenlanders.[119]

However, in the end, after meeting Aslan, Shasta (or Cor as we must now call him) shows true humility. When he meets up again with Aravis, wearing his princely clothes, and bringing with him his royal escort, he doesn't want Aravis to think he is trying to impress her. In fact, he is embarrassed to tell her how his actions have served to fulfill prophecy in the saving of Archenland from Rabadash and his men. Even though Cor very much wants the story of his bravery in facing

---

114 Ibid. p. 19.
115 Ibid. p. 45.
116 Ibid. p. 40.
117 Ibid. p. 73.
118 Ibid. p. 76.
119 Ibid. p. 155.

the Lion to be known, he refuses to tell the story himself. And once the story is told he doesn't enjoy it half as much as he expected.[120]

We are introduced, early on in the story, to Bree's vanity. When Shasta laughs at Bree rolling in the grass, Bree wonders whether he has picked up some bad habit in which talking horses should not engage. Bree is afraid of how he will look to others once he returns to Narnia.[121] Bree's pride shows up again after he fails to help Hwin and Aravis when they are being attacked by Aslan. Bree is so ashamed of himself that he prefers not to go to Narnia rather than have his cowardice become known. The Hermit urges Bree to see that he has lost nothing but his self-conceit. If Bree will recognize that he is not the great war-horse he once thought he was then he can become a decent horse indeed.[122] Of course, for Bree, like the others, it will require a meeting with Aslan to bring about this transformation. In fact, Bree's vanity continues to show itself right up until his encounter with Aslan.[123]

We must remember that Lewis does not draw each character in the Narnian stories as though they are allegorical representations of various moral qualities. Bree cannot simply be reduced to a foil for showing what vanity is all about. Bree also shows good qualities throughout the story. Bree models the habit of proper listening when Aravis tells her story. He is, on the whole, respectful of his traveling companions. He shows a certain amount of bravery, in some situations, as well as ingenuity and pluck.

On the whole it would seem that the greatest vice we are warned against in *The Horse and His Boy* is that of pride, and the greatest virtue which is extolled is that of humility. Rabadash is the epitome of self-centeredness[124] and pride,[125] though he does seem to change, internally, after Aslan turns him, externally, into a donkey.[126] Lasaraleen, too, is an example of a self-involved person. She is better at talking than

---

120 Ibid. p. 204.
121 Ibid. p. 20.
122 Ibid. p. 146.
123 Ibid. p. 191.
124 Ibid. p. 64.
125 Ibid. p. 208.
126 Ibid. pp. 212-213.

listening.[127] Her deep selfishness rises to the top when she and Aravis are trapped in the Tisroc's palace and in danger of discovery. She is more concerned about hiding herself than saving Aravis.[128] Aravis too, like Bree and Rabadash and Lasaraleen, is proud. But she is also true to her friends.[129] And after her encounter with Aslan she becomes a humbler sort of person. She realizes how she has been snubbing and looking down on Shasta, and how Shasta is really the best of them all. She recognizes it is better to say she is sorry than to go back to the old life she once had.[130]

The Beauty of Creation

Another thing we see along the journey with Shasta, Bree, Aravis and Hwin is the beauty of Aslan's creation. There are a couple of references in *The Horse and His Boy* to the country being better than the city. When Shasta gets out of Tashbaan he revels in the clear running water which is delightfully fresh after the smell and heat of the city.[131] We are also told that Aravis used to live in the country and that, even in her old life, she hated every minute of her time in Tashbaan.[132]

Lewis' love of the sea is powerfully present in this story, if only for brief moments. One of the most beautiful descriptions of Aslan's creation is given early in *The Horse and His Boy*. Shasta and Bree come to a place where the turf is intermingled with white flowers and slopes down to the edge of a cliff. Far below them is the sea with the faint sound of breaking waves. We are told that Shasta had never seen the sea from such a height before, nor had he seen so much of it, nor dreamed how many colors there were in it. On either side of Shasta and Bree the coast stretches away, headland after headland; they can see white foam running up the rocks in the distance but making no noise because it is too far off for them to hear. There are seagulls flying overhead and the heat shivers on the ground for it promises to be a blazing hot day.[133]

---

127 Ibid. p. 95.
128 Ibid. p. 103.
129 Ibid. p. 81.
130 Ibid. p. 146.
131 Ibid. p. 79.
132 Ibid. p. 121.
133 Ibid. p. 18.

C. S. Lewis loved the ocean. His mother would take him, and his brother Warren, on holiday to the Antrim Coast north of Belfast when they were small children. Jack and Warnie, as they were both known to family and friends, crossed the Irish Sea on the ferry as many as six times every year when they would travel from their home in Belfast to boarding school in England and back again. Jack loved Northern Ireland so much that he spent many vacations there as an adult, quite often staying at The Old Inn at Crawfordsburn, a short walk away from the sea.

Much of the landscape of Narnia is reminiscent of Ireland. In particular, the tombs of the ancient kings outside of Tashbaan, built to look like stone bee-hives, are very like the ancient bee-hive looking huts along the west coast of Ireland.

Lewis enables us to feel Shasta's enjoyment of nature at certain points in the story. When Shasta is waiting for his traveling companions by the tombs we read that he goes down to the river to have a drink. The water is so pleasant that he takes off his hot, dirty clothes and goes for a swim. When he comes out he lies on the grass for a few minutes and just exults in the pleasure of it all.[134]

After their long sojourn across the desert, the four travelers come to a place where a little cataract of water from a stream is pouring into a broad pool. Both the horses quickly make their way into the pool with heads down, drinking in as much as they can. And Shasta plunges in, stooping his head right into the cataract. Lewis tells us that it was perhaps the loveliest moment in Shasta's life.[135]

Once on a journey to Scotland the Lewis brothers spent a glorious hour beside a golden brown mountain stream with cataracts and deep pools. Jack wrote of the occasion that he and his brother spread out all their sweaty clothes to dry on the flat stones. They lay down together in a pool just under a little waterfall, and let the foam run down the back of their heads and around their necks. Then when they were cool, they came out and sat naked to eat their sandwiches, with their feet still in the rushing water.[136] As Lewis' biographer, George Sayer,

---
134 Ibid. p. 87.
135 Ibid. p. 128.
136 Hooper, Walter, ed., *They Stand Together: The Letters of C. S. Lewis to Arthur*

comments: "Jack's enjoyment of such scenes was as great as that of the most romantic of the romantic poets."[137]

As the travelers in *The Horse and His Boy* near the home of the Hermit of the Southern March, Shasta begins to appreciate the new landscape of the North. There are steep hills, open park-like country with no roads nor houses, and scattered trees everywhere. Rabbits scurry about and the travelers get to see a herd of fallow deer. We are told that Shasta, who had spent his whole life in an almost tree-less grassland, had never seen so many trees, nor so many kinds of trees.[138] There is a love of trees expressed throughout *The Chronicles of Narnia*. This reveals that Lewis had almost as deep a love of trees as his friend J. R. R. Tolkien.[139]

Servant Leadership

Another lesson we learn along the journey in *The Horse and His Boy* is about servant leadership. We are introduced to a false sort of hierarchy or kingship in the form of the Tisroc, who must always be treated with a sort of deified reverence by his subjects. Bree recognizes this as false worship and refuses to engage in such talk, which he says is only fit for slaves and fools. There is a false hierarchy in Calormen because the Calormenes serve a false god, Tash, who is "irresistible and inexorable".[140] Lewis seems to take great joy in poking fun at the pompously hierarchical society of Tashbaan in which you have to bow and scrape before your superiors.

However, with the introduction of the Narnians into the story we are presented with a vision of true and right hierarchy. The Narnian nobles do not ride on litters, but walk along like everyone else. Instead of being grave and mysterious like the Calormene nobles, the

---

Greeves (1914-1963), New York: Macmillan, 1979, [Aug. 17th 1933] p. 456.
137 Sayer, George, *Jack: A Life of C. S. Lewis*, Wheaton, Illinois: Crossway, 1994, pp. 246-247.
138 *The Horse and His Boy*, pp. 134-135.
139 The last photograph of J. R. R. Tolkien was taken next to one of his favorite trees, the Pinus Nigra, in the Botanic Garden in Oxford, England on August 9, 1973. See photos in Carpenter, Humphrey, *Tolkien: A Biography*, Boston: Houghton Mifflin Company, 1977.
140 There seems to be a similaritiy between the Calormene religion and the fatalism of Islam.

Narnians walk with a swing.[141] Lewis builds in the reader a delight in all things Narnian by showing the contrasting silliness of Calormene ways, in particular, the constant Calormene habit of quoting proverbs! Calormene poetry is very dull and practical whereas Narnian poetry is highly romantic. Even Aravis comes to detest the false hierarchy of Calormen.

In Shasta we come to see what true nobility, and bravery, is all about. Shasta's faithfulness to protect Aravis and Hwin leads to him being given the larger task of warning King Lune of Rabadash's intended attack. Toward the end of *The Horse and His Boy* it is recognized that there is something different about Shasta. After Shasta tries to rescue Aravis and Hwin from the lion's attack, at the risk of his own life and limb, both Bree and Hwin acknowledge that Shasta is the best of them all.[142] A little later, the Lord Darrin, seeing how Shasta takes his seat on a horse, recognizes that there must be noble blood in him.[143] But when Shasta does realize that his father is King Lune, he wears his royalty lightly.

King Lune, in the end, describes what proper hierarchy, servant kingship, is all about. He says that to be a king is to be the first person in every attack and the last person in retreat. When there is hunger in the land the king must wear finer clothes and laugh louder over a skimpier meal than any person in his kingdom.[144]

To Lewis' mind, the proper king is one who acts as a servant. This was Lewis' belief because our divine monarch, the Lord Jesus Christ, had a servant's heart and washed his disciples' feet. Jesus said, "For even the Son of Man did not come to be served, but to serve, and to give his life as a ransom for many."[145] Clearly for Lewis, the greatest in the kingdom is the least of all, the servant of all. The greatest king is the one who is most humble, most serving, most loving.

---

141 *The Horse and His Boy*, pp. 54-55.
142 Ibid., p. 151.
143 Ibid., p. 156.
144 Ibid. p. 215.
145 Mark 10:45.

Seeing Aslan Afresh

Of course, the King of kings in Narnia is the great lion, Aslan. Along the journey we are introduced to Aslan through the fresh eyes of Shasta, Bree, Aravis and Hwin, who have never met Aslan before.

The most moving personal encounter in *The Horse and His Boy* is between Shasta and Aslan.[146] It is dark and Shasta is alone and tired, traipsing across the countryside on his horse after warning King Lune of the impending attack on Anvard by Rabadash. Suddenly Shasta realizes that there is some Thing beside him. "Who are you?" Shasta asks. By breathing on Shasta, the Thing assures him that he is not a ghost. The Thing tells Shasta that he is a lion, the Lion who has been watching over Shasta and caring for him all through his young life. Again Shasta asks, "Who *are* you?" The Voice responds, "Myself." very deep and low so that the earth shakes. Then the Voice says again, "Myself." loud and clear and happy. And then a third time he says, "Myself." whispered so softly that Shasta can hardly hear it, and yet it seems to come from all round him as if the leaves rustled with the Voice. Is there an echo here of the gentle whisper with which Yahweh spoke to Elijah in 1 Kings 19? Is there not a hint of the three-fold name of God[147] who is thrice holy?[148]

The night is turning to morning and Shasta sees a golden light falling on them from the left. He thinks it is the sun, but he turns and sees a huge Lion from whom the light is coming. After one glance at the Lion's face Shasta dismounts and falls at the Lion's feet. The High King above all kings stoops toward him. Its mane, and some strange and solemn perfume that hangs about the mane, is all around Shasta. The Lion touches Shasta's forehead with its tongue. He lifts his face and their eyes meet. Then instantly the pale brightness of the mist and the fiery brightness of the Lion roll themselves together into a swirling glory and gather themselves up and disappear.[149]

In this encounter we get Lewis' powerful picture of what it might be like to meet God. Aslan invites Shasta to tell him his sorrows. Then

---

146 *The Horse and His Boy*, p. 441.
147 Matthew 28:19.
148 Isaiah 6:3.
149 *The Horse and His Boy*, pp. 163-166.

Aslan tells Shasta *his* story, but refuses to tell Shasta Aravis's story. This is Lewis' masterful way of showing us how God deals with our "why" questions. God doesn't tell us other people's stories. We can't understand why certain things happen in our *own* stories until we read them in the context of Aslan's *whole* story. Be that as it may, as a result of meeting Aslan Shasta finds that fear is compatible with joy; he receives light on the pathway of his journey; and he drinks living water flowing from Aslan's footprint.[150]

After Shasta's encounter with Aslan we are treated to three encounters between Aslan and Hwin, Bree and Aravis respectively. As already mentioned, Hwin is the quickest to come to Aslan when he meets all three sojourners. Bree is the one who does not believe that Aslan is a true beast, until he meets him. Aslan invites Bree to draw near to him and see that he is indeed a true beast. This reminds us of the fact that Christ is true man as well as true God. Then, after greeting Hwin and Bree, Aslan invites Aravis to draw near to him. He promises not to scratch her this time. Aslan explains to Aravis why he had to scratch her the first time.

Perhaps the most entertaining encounter is that between Aslan and Rabadash. Aslan warns Rabadash that his doom is near. He urges Rabadash to forget his pride and anger, and to accept the mercy of King Lune and King Edmund. But despite Aslan's warnings Rabadash continues to hold on to his desire to take Susan back to Tashbaan with him. Finally, Aslan turns Rabadash into a donkey. But even after this punishment Aslan tells Rabadash that he will not always be an ass, if he is careful to follow Aslan's instructions, which include going to the temple of Tash for healing and staying within ten miles of Tashbaan for the rest of his life.

In this encounter between Aslan and Rabadash, Lewis shows us the almost unlimited patience of Christ, the gentle strength of Jesus, God's justice mixed with mercy. The Lord gives us many opportunities to turn to him in repentance. But those opportunities will not go on forever. As Lewis says in *The Problem of Pain*, if a million chances for repentance were likely to help, they would be given. But a teacher often knows, when students and their parents do not, that it is really useless

---

150 Ibid. p. 161.

to give a student another try at a certain examination. Finality must come sometime, and God, as the master teacher, knows when enough is enough.[151]

Sometimes, sadly, the Lord gives us humans exactly what we ask for, just as Aslan gave Rabadash the opportunity to be healed, but only in the temple of Tash to whom Rabadash had appealed. It makes one wonder, what blessings did Rabadash forfeit by not begging Aslan himself for mercy?

Providence

In sum, *The Horse and His Boy* is a story about the providence of Aslan. The reality of luck is denied throughout the book. As the Hermit says, he has lived a hundred and nine years in this world and has never yet encountered any such thing as luck.[152]

Shasta remarks to himself about his incredible luck at finding the pass between Archenland and Narnia in the middle of the night. Then he realizes it wasn't luck at all, rather it was the guidance of Aslan that pointed him through in the right direction.[153]

Aslan gives us a picture of Christ as the one who sustains his people. He is the one behind all the stories.[154] Aslan is the lion who forces Shasta to join with Aravis. He is the cat who comforts Shasta among the tombs. He is the lion who drives the jackals away from Shasta while he sleeps. He is the lion who gives the horses the new strength of fear for the last mile so that Shasta reaches King Lune in time. And Aslan is the lion Shasta does not even remember who pushed the boat in which he lay, a child near death, so that it came to shore where a man sat, wakeful at midnight, to receive him.[155] It could be argued that "Guide" is the predominant role of Aslan throughout *The Chronicles of Narnia*, even when he is not a visible part of much of the action. Even in those times, Aslan is still playing the most crucial role,

---

151 *The Problem of Pain*, p. 124.
152 *The Horse and His Boy*, p. 143.
153 Ibid. pp. 162,176.
154 Ibid. p. 199.
155 Ibid., p. 158.

behind the scenes, guiding each character who is one of his followers and providing for their needs.

In the next story, we move hundreds of years ahead in Narnian history, but we will see Aslan once again as the one who sustains his people, even in the midst of very dark times. For Aslan is the one who brings restoration after corruption.

Discussion Questions

1. Does this story feel the same, or different, to you than the other Narnia tales? Why?
2. What do you think of Lewis' descriptions of nature in this story? Is there one passage you particularly like?
3. How does "calling and conversion" take place in each of the major characters in this story?
4. How did you react to Shasta's meeting with Aslan? What does this encounter reveal about Aslan?
5. What do you think of Aslan's explanation to Aravis about his wounding her? How do you respond to the fact that Aslan tells no one any story but their own?
6. How do you respond to Aslan's dealing with Rabadash? Does it surprise you in any way?
7. In what way is Aslan at the back of all the stories?

IV. Restoring True Religion after a Corruption
Prince Caspian

Our Time, Narnian Time & Beyond Time

One of the most intriguing aspects of the Narnia stories, which first appears in *The Lion, the Witch and the Wardrobe* and then appears again in *Prince Caspian,* is the difference in time between our world and Narnia. When Lucy first enters Narnia and spends hours and hours with Mr. Tumnus, she then returns to our world where no time has passed at all. Lucy's siblings think she is crazy, or silly, or making up a story about being in another country for hours on end, because her siblings know that no time has passed whatsoever.

The professor, on the other hand, sees the difference in time as a reason for believing Lucy's story to be true. He states that he would not be surprised to find that if Lucy got into another world, that world would have a separate time. On the other hand, it doesn't seem likely that a girl Lucy's age would make up the idea of a different time frame. If she was pretending, and wanted to put something over on her siblings, she would have hidden for an appropriate amount of time and then come out to tell her story.[156] Of course, the other reason why the professor believed Lucy's story, is because he, Professor Digory Kirke, had been to Narnia himself when he was just a boy, as related in *The Magician's Nephew.*

We meet this quirkiness about time again at the beginning of *Prince Caspian.* Lewis reminds us that while the Pevensies were in Narnia the first time they seemed to reign for years and years, but when they returned to our world it all seemed to have taken no time at

---
156 *The Lion, the Witch and the Wardrobe*, p. 46.

all. Now, in *Prince Caspian,* one year of our time has passed since the events of *The Lion, the Witch and the Wardrobe.* The Pevensies return to Narnia, but in this instance time has worked differently; only one year of our time has passed while hundreds of years of Narnian time have elapsed. After discovering the ruins of Cair Paravel, and thinking about the whole situation, the Pevensies realize that they are coming back to Narnia as if they were Crusaders or Anglo Saxons or Ancient Britons coming back to modern England.

While the quirkiness about time is, for Lewis, a literary device, it also ties in to some things he says elsewhere about time. In *Mere Christianity* Lewis has a chapter entitled "Time and Beyond Time". In that chapter Lewis makes the point that God is outside of time, just as a person writing a novel is outside of the time sequence of the novel. The difference is that with the human author he or she leaves one time sequence (that of the novel) to enter another time sequence (that of our own world). However, God is outside of all time sequences.

This idea, of God being outside of time, answers a few difficulties:

Difficulty #1: How does God have time to listen to everyone's prayers? Answer: God doesn't have to listen to everyone's prayers in just one snippet of time. Lewis notes how God has "forever" in which to listen to the instantaneous prayer made by a pilot as his plane crashes in flames.[157]

Difficulty #2: How did the whole universe keep going while Christ was a baby, or while he was asleep? Answer: the time sequence of the life of Christ can't be fit into any time sequence of the life of God. Christians believe that God has put himself as a character into this novel we know as human history, and we call that character Jesus of Nazareth. A novelist who puts himself as a character into his own novel can be doing all sorts of things in real time while his character in the novel can be doing completely different things in the time sequence of the novel. The same is true of God in relationship to Christ.

Difficulty #3: If God knows what I am going to do tomorrow then how can I be free to do otherwise? Again, the problem comes

---

157 *Mere Christianity,* p. 146.

from believing that God is in the same time-sequence that we are in as human beings. But if God is outside of time then we shouldn't properly talk about him *foreseeing* our future acts. He merely *sees* what we are doing when we do it. Our actions at each moment are no less free because God sees us doing them.

In *Mere Christianity* Lewis says that it is the theologians who started the idea that some things are not in time at all and then the philosophers took over this idea.[158] Lewis was certainly influenced in his concept of God's sovereignty and human free will in relation to time by the writing of a man who was both a Christian and a philosopher: the medieval Roman, Anicius Boethius, who lived from A.D. 480 to 524 or 525. Lewis once noted that Boethius' *Consolation of Philosophy* was one of the ten books which influenced his thinking the most.[159] In that book Boethius writes:

> If you wish to consider, then, the foreknowledge or prevision by which He [God] discovers all things, it will be more correct to think of it not as a kind of foreknowledge of the future, but as the knowledge of a never ending presence. . . . God sees all things in His eternal present. . . . God sees those future events which happen of free will as present events; so that these things when considered with reference to God's sight of them do happen necessarily as a result of the condition of divine knowledge; but when considered in themselves they do not lose the absolute freedom of their nature. All things, therefore, whose future occurrence is known to God, do without doubt happen, but some of them are the result of free will.[160]

In *Reflections on the Psalms*, Lewis also cites Plato and the Bible as sources for the idea that God is outside of time. Psalm 90:4 talks about a thousand years being like a single day to God, and 2 Peter 3:8 says that one day is as a thousand years. Lewis posits that the Psalmist probably meant that God is everlasting, that God's life is infinite in time. But Peter takes God out of the time-series altogether. Lewis notes

---

158 Ibid.
159 For a commentary on Boethius by Lewis see Lewis, C. S., *The Discarded Image*, Cambridge: Cambridge University Press, 1964, pp. 75-90.
160 Watts, Victor, translator, Boethius: *The Consolation of Philosophy*, London: Penguin Books, 1999, pp. 134-136.

that Plato had reached this same idea before Peter's Second Epistle.[161] Lewis goes on to say that the eternal may meet us in a day, or a minute or a second. And this raises our hope to finally emerge, if not altogether from time, at least from the tyranny of time. Lewis points out that: human beings are so little reconciled to time that they are astonished by it. We say things like: How John has grown! Or: How time flies! Lewis compares our astonishment at time to the astonishment of a fish at being surrounded by water. A fish surprised by the wetness of water would be very strange, unless that fish were destined to become a land animal.[162] So Lewis suggests that we, as human beings, are destined one day to live, if not outside of time, at least outside the pressure of time. Lewis gives us a glimpse of what this time-free life will be like at the end of *The Last Battle*.

The wonderful thing to see in this is that Lewis' writings were all of a piece. His studies in philosophy informed his writing of children's stories. And the reading of his children's stories can lead out, in time, to a reading and understanding of Lewis' philosophy and theology.

Nostalgia

One of the most delightful things about *Prince Caspian* is the spirit of nostalgia and discovery at the beginning of the story. Nostalgia is really just one aspect of *Sehnsucht*. Nostalgia is a longing, but a particular kind of longing. It is a longing to return to some past period or irrecoverable condition. The Pevensie's discovery of the ruins of Cair Paravel makes them want to return to the time when they all reigned as kings and queens in Narnia.

Lewis uses this aspect of his plot to raise in his readers a sense of longing. But longing for what? Webster defines nostalgia as a kind of homesickness. When we feel a sense of nostalgia are we longing for

---

161 "When the Father who begat the world saw the image which he had made of the Eternal Gods, moving and living, he rejoiced; and in his joy resolved, since the archtype was eternal, to make the creature eternal as far as this was possible. Wherefore he made an image of eternity which is time, having a uniform motion according to number, parted into months and days and years, and also having greater divisions of past, present and future." (Plato, *Timaeus*, 37-38) Plato lived from about 428-348 BC.

162 *Reflections on the Psalms*, pp. 137-138.

our real home? In his sermon, *The Weight of Glory*, Lewis says that if we are made for heaven, the desire for our real home will already be in us. Lewis claims shyness in speaking of this desire for our own hidden country. He feels he is almost committing an indecency. For he realizes he is trying to rip open the inconsolable longing in each of his hearers. This longing is something we cannot hide and cannot fully declare either. We cannot declare it because it is a desire for something which has never actually happened in our experience of this world.[163]

Lewis remarks how Wordsworth identified the thing he longed for with certain moments in his past.[164] But, Lewis insists, this is a cheat. If Wordsworth, or any of us, actually went back to the thing in our past which we think we are longing for (Cair Paravel or whatever) we would find that this was not the thing itself but only a reminder of the thing we really long for, which is heaven.

In his sermons, stories and other pieces of writing, Lewis tries to weave a spell. However, he insists it is a spell not for inducing an enchantment, but for breaking it. He asserts that we are all in need of the strongest spell possible in order to break the evil enchantment of worldliness, an attachment solely to this natural world, which has hung over humanity for over a hundred years. In short, through the Narnia stories as well as his other works, Lewis tries to awaken in the reader a desire for the supernatural realm. In *Prince Caspian* Lewis seeks to rouse this desire in us through the spell of nostalgia.

The Old & the New

In *Prince Caspian* there is an opposition between the old and the new. There are the Old Narnians, that is the talking animals along with

---

163 *The Weight of Glory*, pp. 6-7.
164 See especially William Wordsworth, *Ode: Intimations of Immortality* and *The Prelude*. Lewis was once asked, "What books did most to shape your vocational attitude and your philosophy of life?" Lewis answered with the following list: *Phantastes* by George MacDonald, *The Everlasting Man* by G. K. Chesterton, *The Aeneid* by Virgil, *The Temple* by George Herbert, *The Prelude* by William Wordsworth, *The Idea of the Holy* by Rudolf Otto, *The Consolation of Philosophy* by Boethius, *Life of Samuel Johnson* by James Boswell; *Descent into Hell* by Charles Williams, and *Theism and Humanism* by Arthur James Balfour. (This list first appeared in *The Christian Century*, June 6, 1962.)

other creatures, and then there are the New Narnians, the Telmarines, represented by Miraz the usurper.[165] The New Narnians, under Miraz, have sought to wipe out the memory of Old Narnia because they, the New Narnians, want to be in absolute control of the land. It is the New Narnians who have silenced the beasts, the trees and the fountains. The New Narnians are at war with all wild things. Miraz is afraid of any talk about Aslan because he is afraid of the supernatural, afraid of anything more powerful than himself. Miraz wants to be in control of Narnia instead of Aslan.

There is another distinction among the Old Narnians. Among the Old Narnians there are those who believe in Aslan, like Trufflehunter the badger, but there are also those like Trumpkin and Nikabrik who do not believe. Even between Trumpkin and Nikabrik there is a distinction. Nikabrik believes in the supernatural realm, but he doesn't much care where his practical help comes from, the good side or the evil.[166] Trumpkin is a skeptic about both, he generally believes only in what he can see, hear, touch, taste and smell, though he is open to the possibility that the supernatural realm may exist, and he is open to reason, as his encounter with the Pevensies proves. Among the New Narnians most do not seem to believe in the supernatural realm at all. Or like Miraz, they are trying to wipe out the memory of it. There are a few, like Caspian's nurse and the half-breed Dr Cornelius, who are attempting, surreptitiously, to spread the knowledge of Old Narnia, but they are in the distinct minority. Interestingly enough, the New

---

165 In Miraz, who calls himself Lord Protector, I believe we are meant to see a type of Cromwell who supplants the rightful monarchy. There is a strong emphasis throughout *Prince Caspian* on true kingship versus false leadership. There is a clear delineation of hierarchy and the manner in which commoners should relate to those of royal blood. When Dr Cornelius tells Prince Caspian that he is the true King of Narnia, the true son and heir of Caspian the Ninth, Cornelius, to Caspian's great surprise, drops down on one knee and kisses his hand.

166 Trufflehunter, the true believer, gives Nikabrik, the pragmatist, an important warning. He warns Nikabrik that they will not have Aslan for their friend if they trust in evil spirits. This warning is reminiscent of that in Scripture: "You adulterous people, don't you know that friendship with the world is hatred toward God? Anyone who chooses to be a friend of the world becomes an enemy of God." (James 4:4)

Narnians, like Caspian, who believe in Old Narnia and love "the Old Things", do not simply believe in the existence of talking animals, they believe in the existence of Aslan as well. The two beliefs are woven together into one whole.

This aspect of *Prince Caspian* corresponds to a larger theme within the Lewis corpus. In his inaugural lecture as Professor of Medieval and Renaissance English Literature at Cambridge, Lewis refers to himself as "Old Western Man".[167] In that lecture Lewis argues that the greatest divide in human history took place somewhere between the time of Jane Austen and Sir Walter Scott and our own time, that is between about 1820 and now. Lewis maintains that no one can point to a particular year or decade in which this change began, and he allows that in his own time the change is not yet complete. Therefore, Lewis insists that in his own time people who really could be categorized on different sides of the divide are actually co-mingling. Lewis styles himself as "Old Western Man" and places his students on the new side of the divide.

Lewis notes four areas of change between the time of Austen/Scott and our own: in politics, in the arts, in religion, and in technology. The most interesting change which Lewis notes, in terms of our purpose here, is in the area of religion. He calls it the un-christening of Europe. He allows that certainly there were religious skeptics in Jane Austen's time, just as there are true believers in our time. But the presumption has changed. In the time of Austen and Scott some kind and degree of religious belief was the norm. Not so in Lewis' day. And he goes even further. He suggests that the pagan and the Christian have much more in common with each other than the post-Christian has with the pagan or the Christian.

Returning to Narnia, we see that the corruption of Narnia is typified by the fact that many beasts have become enemies of the true Narnia and have lost their ability to speak.[168] The tricky thing is that there are still some of the talking beasts left. So one never knows for certain which is which, as in the case of the bear which Trumpkin shoots. Lucy remarks to Susan about how awful it would be if some

---

167 Lewis, C. S., *They Asked for a Paper*, London: Geoffrey Bles, 1962, pp. 9-25.
168 Lewis, C. S., *Prince Caspian*, New York: Macmillan, 1973, p. 116.

day in our own world human beings started going wild inside, like the animals in Narnia. What if they still looked human, but you never knew which humans were wild and which ones were still fully human?[169]

This is exactly the situation Lewis predicted would happen in his book *The Abolition of Man*. He foresaw a time when human beings, stepping outside the *Tao*, outside morality, would step into the void, when man's final conquest would prove to be the abolition of man.[170]

Old Narnia corresponds, in a way, to Old Western Europe – an age of rulers rather than leaders, a period of intelligible art rather than unintelligible, a time of traditional moral categories rather than artificial conditioning, an era of faith rather than unbelief, an age before machines as opposed to the ugliness of industrialism. Most importantly, *Prince Caspian* is about "the restoration of the true religion after a corruption". And so *Prince Caspian* suggests to us how true religious belief might be restored in our own post-Christian age.

How Narnia is Restored

The means by which the Kings and Queens of old are brought back to Narnia is the blowing of Queen Susan's magic horn. So, in a sense, by an act of prayer, help is sought and attained. It is also significant that the act of blowing Queen Susan's horn is done at sunrise, just as many significant times of prayer in the Bible are performed at daybreak.[171] The Pevensies feel a bit queer at being called up like this. Edmund remarks at how uncomfortable it is to know that one can be beckoned like that.[172]

Lewis himself knew the strange feeling of being summoned by prayer. In an essay entitled "The Efficacy of Prayer" Lewis wrote about a day when he was intending to have his hair cut in preparation for a visit to London. The first letter he opened that day made it apparent he was not needed in London. So he decided to put off the haircut. However, Lewis had a nagging thought in his mind, almost like a voice

---

169 Ibid. p. 117.
170 *The Abolition of Man*, p. 77.
171 See Genesis 19:27; 28:18; Exodus 24:4; 34:4; 1 Samuel 1:19; Job 1:5; Psalm 5:3; Mark 1:35.
172 *Prince Caspian*, p. 96.

telling him to go get his hair cut anyway. In the end he couldn't stand it any longer. He went for the haircut, only to find that his barber had been praying that Lewis would come by that day. The barber was a man of many problems whom the Lewis brothers had been able to help from time to time. Lewis found that if he had come for a haircut a day later he would have been of no use to his barber in his time of need. The whole experience filled Lewis with a sense of awe.[173]

Obedience to proper authority is another important principle of restoration taught in *Prince Caspian*. Trumpkin, even though he doesn't believe in the power of the horn, offers to go to Cair Paravel and wait for the help which may come. Trumpkin gives to Caspian his reason: He confesses that Caspian is his king and that he knows the difference between giving advice and obeying orders. Having given his advice, Trumpkin is now ready to obey Caspian's command.[174]

Another key to restoration is faith. It is the faith of Lucy which leads the children to Aslan, and thence to Aslan's How, [175] in time to rescue Prince Caspian and start setting things right. It is Lucy, as the youngest, who is the first to see Aslan upon the Pevensies' return to Narnia. As Jesus said, "I tell you the truth, unless you change and become like little children, you will never enter the kingdom of heaven."[176] Characteristically, Aslan is leading Lucy to go the way which is opposite to the course the others want to take. "'For my thoughts are not your thoughts, neither are your ways my ways.' declares the Lord."[177] Trumpkin the skeptic cannot comprehend the vision of faith which Lucy has. And so Peter asserts that Trumpkin must simply accept that the Pevensies do really know about Aslan, at least a little bit about him.[178]

---

173 Lewis, C. S., *The World's Last Night*, San Diego: Harcourt Brace & Company, 1987, p. 3.
174 *Prince Caspian*, p. 92.
175 Aslan's How, according to Dr Cornelius, is a mound which the Old Narnians raised in ancient times over a very magical place where stands the Stone Table. In this sense Aslan's How is like the Church of the Holy Sepulchre in Jerusalem, raised over the site of Jesus' crucifixion and resurrection.
176 Matthew 18:3.
177 Isaiah 55:8.
178 *Prince Caspian*, p. 122.

Lewis shows us in *Prince Caspian* that the solution to the impasse between faith and unbelief is not democracy. The key to restoring Narnia is not to follow majority rule, but rather to follow the vision of faith. When the Pevensies and Trumpkin vote on which direction to go to get to Aslan's How, they end up choosing the wrong direction. They later discover that following Lucy's vision would have been the best thing to do.

Later, Lucy not only has a vision of Aslan, but she *hears* Aslan calling her name in the middle of the night. Lucy ventures out in the dark to find Aslan, only to discover that the spirits of the trees have come alive and are dancing, with Aslan standing in the midst of them. The presence of Aslan brings about the healing of creation. This corresponds to what Paul says in Romans 8:19-21,

> The creation waits in eager expectation for the sons of God to be revealed. For the creation was subjected to frustration, not by its own choice, but by the will of the one who subjected it, in hope that the creation itself will be liberated from its bondage to decay and brought into the glorious freedom of the children of God.

Where Aslan is present there is the Great Dance and the healing of all harms.[179]

After Lucy embraces Aslan she remarks at how he is bigger. Aslan tells her this is because she is older and that every year she grows she will find him bigger. These words communicate the wonderful truth that, yes, we must become like children in order to see the King,[180] but also as we grow in spiritual maturity, rather than comprehending the King, we will only find him larger, more mysterious and more wonderful than ever before.

Aslan assigns to Lucy the hard task of waking the others up and inviting them to follow him.[181] Lucy realizes this time that the others

---

179 *The Great Dance* is a frequent image in Lewis' writing. Lewis takes this expression from Gregory of Nazianzus, who used the phrase to refer to relationships in the Trinity. For more on *the Great Dance* see *Mere Theology*, pp. 16, 45-46, 73, 111, 124, 142, 145, 211, 219, 232.
180 See Matthew 18:3.
181 So too do Christians today have the difficult task of inviting others to follow

still may not see Aslan as she does, and she knows that she must follow Aslan regardless of whether the others do or not. But by burying her head in Aslan's mane Lucy gains new lion-strength for the task at hand. And Aslan assures her that now she is a lioness and all Narnia will be renewed.[182]

Having received the command of Aslan, Lucy goes to her task without pausing to think it through. Lucy's sister and brothers have a hard time understanding why Aslan should be invisible to them. However, in the end, after much fussing and fretting, they follow Lucy, who resolutely fixes her eyes upon Aslan.

Edmund is the next child to have his vision of Aslan restored. At first he sees only Aslan's shadow, like the blind man in the Gospels who needed a second touch from Jesus in order to see fully.[183] Eventually all the children, and Trumpkin, are able to see Aslan, and when they do see him they are filled with a mixture of fear and joy.

The Pevensies' first response to Aslan is to tell him they are sorry for not believing in Lucy's report about him. It is as though the Pevensies are the representative penitent ones whose repentance leads to the restoration of faith in all of Narnia. It takes the breath of Aslan upon Susan to turn her fears to courage again, and it is the breath of Aslan that causes a certain air of greatness to hang about Edmund as he faces the enemy. The breath, or spirit, of Aslan is essential to repentance and the restoration of Narnia.

Trumpkin the skeptic's encounter with Aslan is much more physical than that of the Pevensies. Aslan takes Trumpkin in his mouth, shakes him, throws him up in the air and then catches him with his velveted paws. Then Aslan invites Trumpkin to be friends. The encounter is reminiscent of Thomas the doubter meeting the resurrected Christ. Jesus invites Thomas to put his finger into his nail wounds and his hand into his pierced side. "Stop doubting and believe."[184]

Christ in an age of unbelief.
182 *Prince Caspian*, p. 138.
183 See Mark 8:22-26.
184 John 20:24-29.

Warfare

Of course the most necessary component in the restoration of Narnia is warfare, and not warfare of a merely spiritual kind. In this sense *Prince Caspian* is very much an Old Testament type of story, like Joshua driving the Canaanites out of the Promised Land.

The first battle which takes place is among the Old Narnians themselves. Nikabrik and his rabble of sorcerers must be cleared out of the way before Caspian and the others can effectively take on Miraz. There is no room for division in the ranks. Thus, when it comes to the sticking point, Nikabrik and his crew are killed by Caspian and company.[185] But Lewis gives no countenance to hatred of the enemy. He shows us the right attitude in Caspian's comment about Nikabrik. Caspian says he is sorry for the black dwarf, even though Nikabrik hated him from the beginning. Caspian realizes Nikabrik has gone sour inside from long suffering and hating. He even suggests that if they had won the war with Miraz quickly, Nikabrik might have become a good dwarf in days of peace. Caspian doesn't know who actually killed Nikabrik and he's glad of that. He doesn't relish the thought of killing someone who was once a comrade in arms.[186]

As far as spiritual warfare was concerned, Lewis saw great division in the ranks of Christendom in his day, a division detrimental to the evangelization of the non-Christian world. However, the division Lewis was most concerned about was not the division between denominations, but the division between those who held to a full-bodied supernatural Christianity and those who held to a more watered-down variety. Lewis once wrote in a letter to the *Church Times* that what unites the Evangelical and the Anglo-Catholic, within the Anglican Church, against the liberal or modernist is precisely the fact that the Evangelical and Anglo-Catholic are both thoroughgoing believers in the supernatural. That is, they both believe in the creation, the fall, the incarnation, the resurrection, the second coming, and the

---

[185] It should be obvious from *The Chronicles of Narnia* alone that Lewis was not a pacifist. To understand Lewis' view on this issue one should read, "Why I Am Not A Pacifist" in *The Weight of Glory and Other Addresses*, pp. 33-53. This subject is dealt with in *Mere Theology*, pp. 149-155.

[186] *Prince Caspian*, p.168.

final judgment. According to Lewis, this unites the Evangelical and the Anglo-Catholic not only with each other, but also with Christianity as understood everywhere and by all.[187]

Lewis believed that part of the solution to this problem of confusion in the ranks of Christianity was to more clearly define terms. Therefore Lewis put forward the terms *Deep Church* and Richard Baxter's *mere Christians* as possible labels for all Christian believers in the supernatural realm.[188] Of course, Lewis spent a good part of his life trying to articulate for the world the doctrines of *mere Christianity*. Lewis believed that this was essential to spiritual warfare. Also essential to that warfare was the exposing of the Enemy's plan, which exposé Lewis performed so expertly in the writing of *The Screwtape Letters*.

Returning to Narnia, we see that the next step in the warfare to restore the true religion is to attack the enemy himself. This is where the High King takes charge and challenges Miraz to one-on-one combat. Here the success of the good side is brought about, in part, by the division in the ranks of the evil side–represented by Glozelle and Sopespian, and the pride of Miraz which is his own undoing. In *The Screwtape Letters* Lewis shows us how the pride of Satan and the demons' devouring of one another is also their undoing.[189] The treachery of Glozelle and Sopespian is rewarded with defeat, whereas the honor of the High King is rewarded with victory.

As the coup de grace, Lewis awards the final victory over the Telmarines to the trees which Miraz tried to destroy. Like Birnam Wood moving on Dunsinane to herald the end of Macbeth,[190] so the trees moving on the Telmarines heralds their final defeat. It should be noted that Lewis brings about the defeat of the evil N. I. C. E. in *That Hideous Strength* in a similar manner. The animals on which the operators of the N. I. C. E. have experimented are the ones who turn on their tormentors and eat them alive in the end.[191]

---

187 Lewis, C. S., *God in the Dock*, Grand Rapids: Eerdmans, 1994, p. 336.
188 Ibid.
189 See Lewis, C. S., *The Screwtape Letters*, New York: Macmillan, 1977, [Letter XXXI] pp. 145-149.
190 Shakespeare, William, *The Tragedy of Macbeth*, New York: The New American Library, 1963, [Act V, Scenes III-VIII] pp. 119-131.
191 See Lewis, C. S., *That Hideous Strength*, New York: Simon & Schuster, 1996,

The restoration of Narnia includes the restoration of the land itself to the talking animals, the dwarfs, the dryads, the fauns and other creatures as well as to the humans.[192] We have here a glimpse of Lewis' deep environmental concern which he shared with his friend and fellow author J. R. R. Tolkien. However, Lewis' environmentalism was balanced by a wholesome understanding of humans exercising righteous dominion over creation.[193] As Trufflehunter the Badger says, Narnia is not human beings' country but it is a country for a human being to be sovereign over.[194] Thus, Prince Caspian is made King Caspian of Narnia. And once the restoration of Narnia is complete, the Pevensies, along with those Telmarines who are willing, are sent back to our world through the door in the air created by Aslan.

---

pp. 343-350. Lewis had a great concern both for the unscrupulous destruction of nature, such as took place during the industrialization of Oxford in the early twentieth century, and for unwarranted experimentation with animals. For Lewis' view on the latter please see Lewis' essay on "Vivisection" in *God in the Dock*, pp. 224-228.

192 *Prince Caspian*, p. 207.
193 See Genesis 1:28.
194 *Prince Caspian*, p. 66.

Discussion Questions

1. When the Pevensie children return to Narnia they enter a world where many no longer believe in Aslan. Do you see any parallels in our own world? What do you think Lewis' message is for us in this?
2. Trufflehunter, Trumpkin and Nikabrik each represent different types of people who inhabit a world filled with doubt. How would you characterize each of their approaches to life? With whom do you most identify and why?
3. Lucy's character represents the predicament of believers living in an age of unbelief. What does Aslan ask her to do? What would you do in Lucy's situation?
4. Aslan tells Lucy that every year she grows she will find him bigger. Have you found this to be true in your own relationship with God? If so, how?
5. Trufflehunter says that Narnia is not men's country but it is a country for a man to be king of. At the end of the story, Narnia is given to Caspian as King but also to the talking beasts and other creatures as much as the humans. Do you think Lewis has a message for us in this, about human stewardship of creation? If so, what is that message?
6. Aslan tells Caspian that he is a descendant of Adam and Eve and that this is honor enough to erect the head of the poorest beggar, and shame enough to bow the shoulders of the greatest emperor on earth. What does this tell us about Lewis' understanding of the nature of human beings? Do you agree?
7. What do you think of the violence in *Prince Caspian*? Is it helpful or harmful for children to read stories of this kind?

V. THE SPIRITUAL LIFE
The Voyage of the Dawn Treader

The Voyage of the Dawn Treader, like *The Horse and His Boy*, is another Narnian tale about a journey, only this journey is by sea. Along the way Lewis teaches us, through story, many lessons about the spiritual life, especially through the example of Reepicheep the valiant mouse.

Edmund and Lucy get to return to Narnia in this story whereas their siblings, Peter and Susan, do not, because they are too old. Edmund and Lucy are joined by their infamous cousin, Eustace. The addition of Eustace makes for the best opening line in any of *The Chronicles* – "There was a boy called Eustace Clarence Scrubb, and he almost deserved it".[195]

The Beginning of the Journey

Edmund, Lucy and Eustace enter Narnia through a picture on the wall of Eustace's house. As the children are staring at what Edmund and Lucy take to be a very Narnian ship, all three of them are suddenly sucked into the waves which begin lapping over the edge of the picture frame. In a matter of moments the children find themselves rescued by Edmund and Lucy's old friend Caspian, who is now King of Narnia. They are taken aboard Caspian's ship – the *Dawn Treader*.

Once the children join the *Dawn Treader*'s voyage, one of the first things which happens is that they become enslaved, along with Reepicheep and King Caspian, on the Lone Islands. This occurs due to

---

195 A slightly different statement might be made about the author of *The Chronicles*: There once was a man named Clive Staples Lewis, and he didn't deserve it! Is it any wonder, with a name like Clive Staples, that C. S. Lewis would choose a nickname for himself, even one so improbable as "Jack"?

Caspian's carelessness in leading the troop on a trek across the island of Felimath, not knowing what they might encounter. Thankfully the children are rescued by the Lord Bern, one of the seven lost lords of Narnia whom Caspian has been seeking. Their redemption is accomplished, first by the Lord Bern buying Caspian out of slavery, and then by a direct confrontation with the sniveling Governor Gumpas who rules the Lone Islands in a slovenly, bureaucratic manner.

If *The Voyage of the Dawn Treader* is all about the spiritual life then it is very appropriate that the journey begins with this rescue from slavery, just as the Christian life begins with a rescue from slavery to sin. Just as Caspian and the children learn from this incident not to be so careless again, so too, we as Christians must learn not to offer ourselves again as slaves to sin. As Paul says in Romans 6:16-17,

> Don't you know that when you offer yourselves to someone to obey him as slaves, you are slaves to the one whom you obey – whether you are slaves to sin, which leads to death, or to obedience, which leads to righteousness? But thanks be to God that, though you used to be slaves to sin, you wholeheartedly obeyed the form of teaching to which you were entrusted.

Storm on the Horizon

The second major event of the *Dawn Treader*'s voyage is a fierce storm. The pleasant time after rescue from slavery in Narrowhaven doesn't last. Isn't this, too, the well worn pattern of the Christian life? Times of healing in the ministry of Jesus are followed by a storm on the Sea of Galilee which threatens to drown the disciples. But Jesus is awakened and he calms the storm.[196] In the same way the joy and peace of the new Christian's life is often followed by unwelcome weather. However, we are taught not to think storms in life to be a strange thing:

> Dear friends, do not be surprised at the painful trial you are suffering, as though something strange were happening to you. But rejoice that you participate in the sufferings of Christ, so that you may be overjoyed when his glory is revealed.[197]

---

196 Matthew 8:23-27.
197 1 Peter 4:12-13.

Through the storms on the open sea all those on the *Dawn Treader* learn how to handle difficult times. The same is true in the spiritual life. "We also rejoice in our sufferings, because we know that suffering produces perseverance; perseverance, character; and character, hope."[198]

The Un-Dragoning of Eustace

Though there are other things which happen first on the *Dawn Treader's* voyage, the spiritual journey of life begins, in a sense, with conversion. And of course, the main conversion story in *The Voyage of the Dawn Treader* is that of Eustace Clarence Scrubb.

When we are first introduced to Eustace we get the picture that this is a very self-centered boy indeed. Eustace loves to boss and bully. He finds many ways to give people a hard time. Once he arrives on the *Dawn Treader* there is almost no end to his complaining. The epitome of Eustace's self-centeredness is seen in his keeping a diary, recording all the ways in which he does right, from his perspective, and all the ways the others are doing him wrong on the voyage.

Lewis himself kept a diary at various times in his life up until the advent of his own re-conversion to Christianity.[199] At that time Lewis gave up writing in a journal. In *Surprised by Joy* he tells us why. He says that his conversion to Theism brought with it a significant decrease in the attention he had so long paid to the progress of his own opinions and states of his own mind. Lewis recognizes that for many healthy extroverts self-examination first begins with conversion. For him it was the opposite. Self-examination continued in his life, but at stated intervals, and only for practical purposes. Self-inspection was from then on a duty in Lewis' spiritual life, a discipline, an uncomfortable thing, no longer a hobby or a habit. For Lewis, faith and prayer were the start of extroversion. He was taken out of himself. And he was very thankful for the fact that his conversion led him to give up what he then thought to be the time-wasting and foolish practice of keeping a diary. Lewis notes that even for autobiographical purposes a journal is

---

198 Romans 5:3-4.
199 See Hooper, Walter, ed., *All My Road Before Me: The Diary of C. S. Lewis, 1922-1927*, San Diego: Harcourt Brace Jovanovich, 1992.

not really that useful. One writes down every day what one thinks is important, but of course one doesn't see each day what will truly be important over the long haul.[200]

We are told in Chapter 5, "The Storm and What Came of It", that something happened to Eustace on the mountainous island that made him forget about keeping his diary for a long time. On this island Eustace's selfishness leads him away from work and away from the group. He wanders away from the shore and off into the hills. While lost in the mountains Eustace comes upon a dying dragon, though he doesn't know it is a dragon, for he has read none of the right books! Once the dragon appears in fact to be dead, Eustace finally takes some hesitant steps toward the beast. He goes to the dragon's pool for a drink, and then the rain drives him into the dragon's cave for shelter. Here Eustace discovers the dragon's hoard. He is happy, for the first time in the story, at the thought of what he might do with all the treasure. He slips a diamond bracelet on to his own arm. And then contemplating greedy, dragonish thoughts, Eustace falls asleep on the dragon's hoard. Having done this, Eustace himself turns into a dragon, though at first he is not aware of the fact.

This is reminiscent of the grumbler who becomes a grumble in Lewis' story of a bus ride from hell to heaven, *The Great Divorce*. In that story Lewis comments about a garrulous old woman who has gotten into the habit of grumbling: Wouldn't a little kindness, and rest, and change put her all right? Lewis' character, George MacDonald, responds that this woman was once a grumbler, but the question is whether or not she is *still* a grumbler. Lewis, in the story, says he thinks the answer obvious. MacDonald tells Lewis he is misunderstanding. The question is whether the woman is a grumbler, or merely a grumble. He tells Lewis that if there is a real woman underneath all the grumbling – even the least trace of real humanity left – then she can be brought to life again.[201]

And that is precisely the question in regard to Eustace: Is there still a real boy left underneath all the dragonish thoughts? As the story progresses we discover the answer.

---

200 *Surprised by Joy*, pp. 232-233.
201 Lewis, C. S., *The Great Divorce*, London: Geoffrey Bles, 1945, p. 68.

Once he realizes that he has become a dragon Eustace becomes lonelier than ever before. He is cut off from the human race and he longs to have fellowship with the people he once hated. Presumably seeking that fellowship, Eustace the dragon flies down to the beach between the *Dawn Treader* and his friends. Once the friends discover that the dragon is indeed Eustace, Eustace becomes no end of help, whereas he was no end of trouble before. He brings food from all over the island for the purpose of re-supplying the ship. He even discovers a tall pine tree to serve as a new mast for the *Dawn Treader*. The new pleasure of being liked and liking other people is what keeps Eustace from despair. He even becomes friends with his former enemy, Reepicheep. At the same time, Eustace is now aware of what a nuisance he has been to everyone.

One night, lying awake thinking of all this, Eustace is approached by Aslan who invites Eustace to follow him. Eustace obeys and Aslan leads him to a garden at the top of a mountain. In the middle of this garden there is a well. The well is very wide, with great marble steps going down into it. Eustace longs to get into the bubbling water which he hopes will ease the pain in his arm, but Aslan tells him he must undress before entering. After thinking about it, Eustace realizes Aslan is talking about his dragon-skin, that he must shed his skin before getting into the pool. Eustace scratches off one layer of skin after another, all to no avail. After each layer Eustace finds another layer underneath, as hard and knobby as the one before. Finally Aslan tells Eustace that he will have to let him undress him. Though Eustace is afraid of Aslan's claws he lies down on his back to let Aslan do his work. The very first tear is so deep that it feels like it is going right into Eustace's heart. The pain is excruciating, but Eustace is relieved, all the same, to have the ugly dragon skin removed. Next, Aslan catches hold of Eustace, throws him into the water, which stings for a moment, and suddenly Eustace realizes he has turned into a boy again.

This is a very dramatic picture indeed, in Narnian terms, of Christian baptism.[202] Even the undressing of Eustace is like the undressing of baptismal candidates in the Early Church who would

---

[202] Lewis says there are three things that spread the Christ-life to us: baptism, belief and Holy Communion. (*Mere Christianity*, p. 62.)

descend, naked, into the waters of baptism. Aslan dresses Eustace in new clothes, just as newly baptized believers in the Early Church were dressed in new white garments, and just as the Lord dresses us in the righteousness of Christ. The most important point is that the un-dragoning of Eustace is accomplished by Aslan.

One of the first results of this un-dragoning is that Eustace apologizes to Edmund for being "pretty beastly". Edmund, of course, says not to mention it, for he knows from personal experience what it's like to be a bad person, and to be changed by Aslan. When Eustace asks Edmund if he knows Aslan, Edmund says that Aslan knows him. And that says it all. The spiritual journey begins, continues, and finds its consummation, only because Aslan knows us.

Lewis' final note on the adventures of Eustace is quite a good summary of the Christian life. Lewis as narrator tells us it would be pleasant, and almost true, to say that at the moment of his un-dragoning Eustace was changed. But to be strictly accurate, Eustace only began to be a different person. He had relapses to his old ways of behavior. His spiritual life from then on was a matter, perhaps, of three steps forward, two steps back. There were still many days when Eustace was very tiresome to those around him. But the important thing was that Aslan's cure had begun.[203]

The cure has begun, that is the most that can be said of any of us at the time of conversion. We begin to be different people when we meet Christ for the first time. But there is still much growing to be done. The prodigal has come home, but he still must learn how to live in the father's house once again.

The World, the Flesh & the Devil

If the stripping away of sinful flesh is dealt with in the adventures of Eustace, then the other two members of the ancient evil triumvirate are dealt with in the chapter about two narrow escapes.

After leaving Dragon Island the *Dawn Treader* comes to an uninhabited island where the only thing of worth discovered is a little

---

203 Lewis, C. S., *The Voyage of the Dawn Treader*, New York: Macmillan, 1962, p. 92.

skin boat, or coracle, along with a paddle, both of which will come in handy later in the story. Once again out on the open sea the *Dawn Treader* is pursued by an unknown something which turns out to be something far worse than expected. At first the thing looks like little smooth rocks all in a row. But then the rocks begin to disappear at different intervals. Finally, the thing rears its ugly head, all green and red and purple with gigantic eyes and razor-sharp teeth–a sea serpent. The crew of the *Dawn Treader* tries to fight off the serpent with arrows; Eustace goes at the loathsome lizard, hacking with his sword. At last, Reepicheep comes up with the best suggestion of all: Don't fight! Push! All spare bodies on deck try to give the serpent, who has wrapped his circuitous body around the *Dawn Treader*, the heave-ho. In the end they are successful in resisting the serpent, though not without the loss of the carved dragon-tail stern of the *Dawn Treader*.

The prophet Isaiah referred to the Lord's enemies as a sea serpent, Leviathan, which the Lord will slay with his fierce, great and powerful sword.[204] Revelation 12:9 identifies the serpent with the devil, or Satan, who is thrown out of heaven down to earth and who pursues the Lord's people to make war against them. Since we are at war with the serpent, thankfully Scripture also tells us how to conduct this warfare. James 4:7 says, "Resist the devil, and he will flee from you."[205] Of course this is precisely what the voyagers on the *Dawn Treader* do; they resist the sea serpent and he flees from them.

The next narrow escape for the voyagers takes place on the very next island they reach. Caspian, the Pevensies, Eustace and Reepicheep venture across the island and come upon a sword, a mail-shirt, helmet, dagger and coins, all Narnian in origin and all in the same spot beside a pool of water. As they try to unravel the mystery of who would have left these things behind and why, Eustace begins to stoop down and scoop up some water to drink out of the pool. Suddenly, Lucy and the others see at the bottom of the pool what looks like a golden statue. Caspian contemplates diving in and hauling out the statue and Edmund uses his hunting spear to measure the depth of the pond. However, before

---

204 Isaiah 27:1.
205 See also 1 Peter 5:8-9. And in Matthew 4:1-11 Jesus shows us *how* to resist the serpent and make him flee.

Edmund can lower the spear very far, he loses his grip, for the spear has suddenly become extremely heavy. The group soon realizes that whatever touches this water turns to gold, just as in the Midas story whatever the king touches turns to gold as well.[206] Caspian surmises that the king who owns this island might become the richest king in the world – and so he claims the island as a Narnian possession and names it Goldwater Island. Edmund objects to this, whereupon he and Caspian begin to fight over the matter until they are interrupted by the sight of Aslan crossing the heathery hillside above them. Edmund and Caspian quickly realize their folly and Reepicheep appropriately renames the island – Deathwater.

In this incident we see the tremendous power which greed can exercise over a person – even a person as good as Caspian. Perhaps this is why the Aslan of our own world teaches us:

> Do not love the world or anything in the world. If anyone loves the world, the love of the Father is not in him. For everything in the world – the cravings of sinful man, the lust of his eyes and the boasting of what he has and does – comes not from the Father but from the world. The world and its desires pass away, but the man who does the will of God lives forever.[207]

The Magician's Book

On the Island of the Voices Lucy is conscripted by the Dufflepuds to speak the spell from the magician's book which will make them visible again. In order to save the lives of her compatriots Lucy consents to go upstairs in the magician's house and read the spell from his magic book. The next day Lucy makes her way upstairs and walks cautiously down the long hall, a hall with strange signs painted on each door and even stranger masks hanging on the walls. When she finally reaches the room with the magic book Lucy sees that it is really a room with

---

206 According to some scholars, the Midas myth is based upon a Phrygian King who appears to have lived in the eighth century B.C. A burial site thought to be his was found in Anatolia (modern-day Turkey). For a beautifully illustrated rendition of this story, based upon Nathaniel Hawthorne's retelling of this ancient Greek myth, see Craft, Charlotte, *King Midas and the Golden Touch*, New York: William Morrow, 1999.
207 1 John 2:15-17.

many books, floor to ceiling, some of them very old and very large. The magic book is lying on a reading desk and she opens it to discover that its pages are crisp and smooth, and a delightful smell emanates from it. Each page is very artfully decorated and the spells themselves begin on the very first page.

Lucy starts leafing through the book trying to find the spell to make things that are invisible visible again. But before she comes to that spell she finds another of great interest to her – a beautifying spell to make the one who utters it the most beautiful person in the world. Lucy soon sees pictures of herself appearing on the page, reciting the spell and becoming exquisitely lovely. In the pictures she even becomes more beautiful than her sister Susan, who was always the more physically attractive of the two girls. Just as Lucy decides she is going to say the spell, Aslan appears on the page, growling. This is enough to make Lucy turn the page.

Later she comes to a spell that will allow her to know what her friends think about her. Since she was good and didn't say the beautifying spell Lucy feels entitled to speak the words of this enchantment. She does say the spell, but is sorry in the end to learn what two of her friends back home in England think of her, or at least, what they appear to think of her.

After this Lucy comes to a spell for the refreshment of the spirit. Lucy finds herself reading something more like a story than a spell. However, it is a story which comes so alive for her that she forgets she is reading. At the end of the tale Lucy thinks it is the most wonderful story she has ever heard. She wants to read it again, but she cannot, for part of the magic of the book is that she cannot turn back to read an earlier page again.

Finally, Lucy comes to the spell for making hidden things visible. She reads it through once, and then says the words out loud. Before she has a chance to do anything about it, Lucy hears soft, heavy footsteps in the corridor. She is somewhat fearful of meeting the magician, but then her fear turns to delight when she sees Aslan. She embraces the lion and tells him how good it is of him to come. Aslan tells her he has been there all along, but that she has just made him visible. Then he warns Lucy about the eavesdropping she has been doing on her friends back in England, and he gives her a lesson about misjudging her friends. Lucy then asks if she will ever be able to read the wonderful story from the magic book again. She asks Aslan to tell it to her. And Aslan assures her that he will be telling her the same story for years and years.

What is the story which Aslan will tell to Lucy for many years to come? It is a story about a cup and a sword, a tree and a green hill. In fact it is the story of the Gospel. The cup is the Holy Grail, the sword is perhaps a sword of execution, the green hill is Calvary and the tree is the one on which Jesus dies.

This gives us a clue that the magician's book is, in a sense, like the Bible. The Bible, like the magic book, is full of information both practical and spiritual. The Bible teaches us, like the magic book teaches Lucy, about sin and temptation and evil. But it is also a book which provides spiritual refreshment. And we gather that by reading the Bible and applying it in our lives we can make the Lord visible to others just as Lucy made Aslan visible.

The Bible was, for C. S. Lewis, the most important of all books. He made it a habit to read portions of the Bible every day of his Christian life. When he was reading the New Testament he would often read it in the original Greek language. In the Old Testament the book of Psalms was a favorite, so much so that Lewis wrote a book entitled *Reflections on the Psalms*. Lewis was involved in the late 1950's and early 60's in revising the translation of the Psalms for the *Book of Common Prayer*, and he was also consulted on the translation of the New Testament for the *New English Bible*. The former work he undertook along with T. S. Eliot.[208] Lewis believed that the Bible was indeed – literature taken up to be the vehicle of God's word.[209]

The Dark Island

After leaving the island of the Dufflepuds the *Dawn Treader* comes upon a great darkness hovering over the sea. Entering the blackness is

---

208 Green, Roger Lancelyn and Hooper, Walter, *C. S. Lewis: A Biography*, Glasgow: Collins, 1980, p. 288.
209 *Reflections on the Psalms*, p. 116.

almost like entering a railway tunnel with no light at the end. Everyone on board the ship wants to turn around, but Reepicheep urges them on, saying that before them there is a great adventure and if they turn back it will be an impeachment of their honor.

Caspian orders the ship's three lanterns to be lit as the *Dawn Treader* sails on into the inky night. The entire crew is summoned to battle positions. As they sail forward in the name of Aslan and are encased in blackness, suddenly a voice cries out from the murky deep. It is a voice with such fear in it that all humanity seems to be gone from it, and the voice begs mercy to be taken on board. The person taken aboard has a wild, white face, wilder looking than any man Edmund has ever seen. His hair is a tousled white mess, his face gaunt. Only a few wet rags of clothing hang from his emaciated body. As soon as his feet reach the deck the stranger urges the voyagers to fly from the dark island. When asked why they should fly, the stranger tells them that this is the island where dreams come true.

At first the people of the *Dawn Treader* think: This is the island we have been looking for all our lives. But then they are made to realize that what the stranger means is: this is the island where *nightmares* come true. The crew begins rowing for all they are worth even as their own worst nightmares steal upon them. As the rest of the crew begins to fear that they shall never get out of the blackness, Lucy, leaning on the edge of the fighting top, whispers a prayer to Aslan saying that if ever he loved them he must come and help them now. Lucy begins to feel a little better, and then a tiny speck of light begins to shine in the distance. Soon, in the midst of the beam of light, Lucy sees what turns out to be an albatross. As the bird circles near her, Lucy hears the voice of Aslan telling her to have courage. In time the albatross leads the *Dawn Treader* to safety and Caspian discovers that they have rescued one of the seven lost lords – the Lord Rhoop.

This chapter reminds us that we all go through times of darkness in our spiritual journeys. We are taught that even some who are very close to the Lord must endure a long, dark night of the soul. Who hasn't experienced dreams so horrible that they envelop the human spirit in utter blackness?

Lewis himself suffered throughout his entire life from horrific nightmares, partly as a result of his service in the army during World War I. Thankfully one very good thing came out of Lewis' dreams – that is the character of Aslan himself. For, as was mentioned in the introduction, Aslan was partly the result of some strange dreams C. S. Lewis had been having about lions in the late 1940's.

How are we to handle psychological and spiritual darkness? We are to handle it the same way Lucy did – calling out to Aslan. Even if we can only utter the one word prayer, "Help!" that cry of desperation will be answered. The Lord will send his albatross to guide us toward the light, and he will whisper in our ears the words we most need to hear: Courage, dear heart.

As the Lord said to Joshua, so he says to us: "Be strong and courageous. Do not be terrified; do not be discouraged, for the Lord your God will be with you wherever you go."[210] If we are valiant like Reepicheep we will even have the privilege of rescuing lost lords, lost people once made in the image of God, from the darkness of psychological and spiritual torment. Jesus is the light of the world and like Paul we are called to open the eyes of the blind and turn people from darkness to his light by the power of God.[211]

The Three Sleepers

After the Dark Island the *Dawn Treader*, after many days at sea, comes upon another island, right at sunset. The island has no mountains, but many gentle hills. An attractive smell wafts its way from the land to the *Dawn Treader*. Upon disembarking, Caspian, the children, Reepicheep, and some of the crew members come upon what seems to be a ruin, not far from shore. It is a wide, oblong structure, with a floor of smooth stones, surrounded by grey pillars with no roof. In the midst of this space there stands a long stone table covered with a rich crimson cloth. On either side of the table are carved stone chairs with silk cushions. On the table is laid a sumptuous banquet. The smell of fruit and wine greets the voyagers with a promise of deep bliss.

---

210 Joshua 1:9.
211 See John 12:46; Acts 26:18; 2 Corinthians 4:6; Ephesians 5:8; Colossians 1:13; 1 Peter 2:9.

As the voyagers draw nearer to the table they see at its head, and on either side, three mops of extremely long hair. Reepicheep, running right up the table to the curious masses of hair realizes there are three men attached to the hair, and as everyone else tentatively draws close they detect that these three men are not dead but asleep. The voyagers attempt to wake the men from their sleep, all to no avail – for the sleep is an enchanted one. As the three sleepers mutter various comments in their dreams and as the voyagers examine the men more closely, they discern that the three sleepers are indeed the last three of the seven lost lords.

Next, the hungry voyagers wonder whether they should fall to and partake of the meal on the table. Caspian and the rest conclude that this would not be a good idea, for it seems that the three men have fallen into an enchanted sleep precisely because they have eaten of the banquet. The crew wishes to return to the *Dawn Treader*, but Reepicheep insists on sitting at the table until sunrise, because it is a great mystery and a great adventure. Caspian and the children agree to stay with Reepicheep while the crew returns to the ship.

In the middle of the night, while Caspian and the children are starting to doze, a figure carrying a light comes out of a doorway in the hillside not far from the table. It is a tall and extremely beautiful girl dressed in a long blue dress. As the light shines on the table Lucy notices something she hadn't seen before – an ancient stone knife. The girl then welcomes the travelers to Aslan's table and asks them why they are not eating and drinking.

Caspian tells the girl that they have not partaken for fear of falling into an enchanted sleep. But the girl tells Caspian that the three sleepers have not even eaten of the banquet. When Lucy asks what happened to the three men the girl explains: The three lost lords when they came to the table began to argue about whether they should remain on this island or sail to the end of the world or return to Narnia. One of the lords picked up the stone knife and would have fought with his fellow lords. But this was a thing not to be done and so as his hands closed on the handle of the knife an enchanted sleep fell upon him and his companions.

Eustace asks about the knife of stone and the girl asks the voyagers if any of them recognize it. Lucy says it was a knife like this one which the White Witch used to kill Aslan on the Stone Table long ago. The girl tells the travelers that this is the very same knife.

Edmund asks the girl how they are to know if she is their friend. How are they to know if it is safe to eat the food? The girl tells Edmund that he cannot know, he can only believe, or not.

It takes Reepicheep only a split second to ask for a cup of wine to be poured for him. He pledges a toast to the lady, drinks of the wine and then begins eating of the banquet. In a short while everyone else follows Reepicheep's example.

When the travelers ask the girl why this is called Aslan's table she tells them it is set here at his bidding for the refreshment of voyagers who come this far. When asked how the food keeps, the girl tells the travelers that it is eaten and replenished every day.

In this table we have a beautiful picture of Holy Communion. The rich crimson represents the blood of Aslan shed for traitors like Edmund. The presence of the knife reveals that this table is like unto the Stone Table upon which Aslan was killed. There is rich food and wine to be had. And in the three sleepers there is an echo of Paul's warning to the Corinthians:

> Therefore, whoever eats the bread or drinks the cup of the Lord in an unworthy manner will be guilty of sinning against the body and blood of the Lord. A man ought to examine himself before he eats of the bread and drinks of the cup. For anyone who eats and drinks without recognizing the body of the Lord eats and drinks judgment on himself. That is why many among you are weak and sick, and a number of you have fallen asleep. But if we judged ourselves, we would not come under judgment. When we are judged by the Lord, we are being disciplined so that we will not be condemned with the world.[212]

To C. S. Lewis, partaking of Holy Communion was very important. He believed it to be a mandate of the New Testament that Christians are obligated to take the Sacrament.[213] For Lewis, the Eucharist is

---

212 1 Corinthians 11:27-32.
213 *God in the Dock*, p. 61.

indeed holy for in it Christ is truly hidden.[214] In his early Christian life C. S. Lewis did not think it important to take Communion every week, but he changed his mind about this later and began to take the Sacrament at least weekly.[215]

Lewis gave some advice to his goddaughter, Sarah, before her first Communion. He advised her not to expect that she would have all the feelings she might wish to have. The right feelings may come and they may not. But, Lewis says, don't worry if you don't get them. Feelings aren't what matter. In taking Communion something real happens whether you feel it or not. Taking Communion does one good just as a meal does a hungry person good even if he has a cold which spoils the taste. Lewis assures his goddaughter that the Lord will give her right feelings if he wants to do so. If he does then we must thank him. If he doesn't give us the feelings we would like, then we must simply recognize that he knows best. This, says Lewis, is one of the very few subjects on which he is an expert. For years after becoming a regular communicant he says he had such dull feelings, and he found his attention wandering at the worst times. But, he says, in the last year or two things have begun to come around for him – which goes to show how important it is to obey, regardless of our feelings.[216]

For Lewis, partaking of the Lord's Table was a very important act of the Christian life. He believed that Holy Communion was a sacrament through which a hand from the hidden country touched not only his soul, but his body. That touch eventually became so real to Lewis that he wanted to experience it as often as possible, for as he found, the Sacrament of Holy Communion is a foretaste of heaven.[217]

Journeying to Aslan's Country

Lewis pictures the heaven-bound person in the character of Reepicheep. In a letter to a child, Lewis once wrote that anyone in our world who devotes his whole life to seeking heaven will be like

---

214 *The Weight of Glory*, p. 19.
215 See *Letters*, p. 40.
216 *Letters to Children*, [3 April 1949] p. 26. See also Lewis, C. S., *Letters to Malcolm: Chiefly on Prayer*, [Chapter XIX] pp. 100-105, for more on Lewis' beliefs about Holy Communion.
217 See Matthew 26:29.

Reepicheep.[218] Reepicheep the mouse is the perfect picture of the heaven-bound person, for he is determined to sail to Aslan's country at all cost.

Reepicheep's desire is to journey to the eastern end of the world where he hopes to find Aslan's country. He never feels the ship is getting on fast enough so he spends much of his time sitting near the dragon's head of the vessel staring out at the eastern horizon. This gives us a hint that Reepicheep is journeying to a type of Jerusalem in the east. Actually, he is going in search of a "New Jerusalem".[219] Caspian's ship is the *Dawn Treader*, and so Lewis subtly suggests that we should all be treading east, toward the dawn of a new world.

Morning is an important image in the writing of C. S. Lewis. When John finally gets to his long dreamed of Island in *The Pilgrim's Regress* it is early morning. There is the purity of early morning air mixed with the sharp scent of the sea as John hears waves crashing.[220] In *The Great Divorce* when the bus load from hell (or purgatory) first arrive on the outskirts of heaven, the light and coolness drenching them is like that of summer morning, early morning, a minute or two before sunrise.[221] Later, in the same book, when the lizard of lust is transformed into a mighty stallion and the ghost is transformed into a real man, they go riding off together into the rose brightness of everlasting morning.[222] So it is appropriate that Reepicheep, who is seeking heaven, is being conveyed by the *Dawn Treader*. Reepicheep has a deep desire for heaven and according to Lewis, that longing is a good one.

Lewis wrote frequently about longing for heaven and he defended the desire as an appropriate one. He maintained that a proper desire for heaven is not mere escapism. Rather, it is one of the things a Christian is meant to have. He pointed out that those Christians who have done the most for this world are the ones who have thought most about the next, people like William Wilberforce, who helped abolish the slave trade in the British Empire. Reepicheep is a Narnian example of the

---

218 *Letters to Children*, [May 29th 1954] p. 45.
219 See Revelation 21.
220 Lewis, C. S., *The Pilgrim's Regress*, Grand Rapids: Eerdmans, 1981, p. 170.
221 *The Great Divorce*, p. 26.
222 Ibid. p. 94.

same principle. Because Reepicheep's heart is so earnestly set upon reaching Aslan's country he is the bravest of all his compatriots. As Lewis says elsewhere, aim for heaven and you will get earth along with it; aim for earth and you will get nothing.[223]

Lewis urges that we must keep alive in ourselves the desire for our true country, the one we will not find until after death. We must make it our main purpose to press on to that other country and help others to do the same.[224] This is exactly what Reepicheep does by urging the men of the *Dawn Treader* on in their journey and always remembering the verse that the Dryad spoke over him in his cradle.

> Where sky and water meet,
> Where the waves grow sweet,
> Doubt not, Reepicheep.
> To find all you seek,
> There is the utter East.[225]

Lewis insists that the desire for heaven should also lead the Christian to have a different attitude toward death than the non-Christian. If this life is really a "wandering to find home," why should we not look forward to our arrival?[226] Certainly Reepicheep has this different attitude toward death. When he comes to the point of making his final journey in his coracle, he is not sad, but rather quivering with happiness.[227] Reepicheep looks forward to going over the eastern edge of the world, and to reaching Aslan's country, as the greatest adventure of all.

But what of the children, Edmund, Lucy and Eustace, how are they to reach Aslan's country? When they reach the very end of the world they come to a place where the blue sky meets the green grass almost like a wall. And on that green grass is something so white they can hardly look at it. It is in fact a lamb – a lamb who offers them breakfast. They ask the lamb if this is the way into Aslan's country and

---

223 *Mere Christianity*, p. 118.
224 Ibid., p. 120. See also *The Weight of Glory*, pp. 8-9.
225 *Voyage of the Dawn Treader*, p. 17.
226 Lewis, C. S., *Letters to an American Lady*, Grand Rapids: Eerdmans, 1967, [June 7th 1959] p. 81.
227 *Voyage of the Dawn Treader*, p. 206.

the lamb tells them that the way for them into Aslan's country is from their own world. In fact, there is a way into Aslan's country from all worlds. And, as he says this, the lamb changes into the great lion, Aslan himself.

Lucy immediately asks Aslan to tell them how to get into his country from their own world. And Aslan promises Lucy that he will be telling them all the time. He doesn't promise whether the way will be long or short, but that it lies across a river, and he himself is the great bridge builder.[228]

Lucy despairs when Aslan tells her and Edmund that they shall not be returning to Narnia. She is discouraged at the thought of not seeing Aslan. In response Aslan tells her that she will meet him in our world, but in our world he has another name. Aslan says that the purpose for them coming to Narnia was that by knowing him for a little while in Narnia they might know him better in our own world.

All of these events and statements in the last chapter of *The Voyage of the Dawn Treader* are clues. The lamb who becomes a lion gives us the hint that Aslan is like Jesus, the lamb of God who is also the lion of the tribe of Judah, the one who makes breakfast for his disciples along the shore of Galilee.[229] And in this last chapter of *The Voyage* Lewis reveals his whole purpose for writing *The Chronicles of Narnia*: that by getting to know Aslan in these books, we might know him better in our own world, and be prepared ourselves to go to Aslan's country one day.

---

228 In Latin the word for priest is "pontifex" which literally means "bridge-builder". Aslan, like Christ in our world, is the bridge-builder, the great high priest. (See Hebrews 4:14 ff.)
229 See John 1:29, Revelation 5:5 and John 21.

Discussion Questions

1. How is the spiritual life like a voyage?
2. Who do you think is the main character in *The Voyage of the Dawn Treader*? Why? What does this character have to teach us about the spiritual life?
3. Have you ever experienced a time where you were "enslaved" like the children on the Lone Islands? If so, how were you set free?
4. What meaning does the story of Eustace's un-dragoning have for you?
5. How is our world today like Deathwater Island? How can we escape its allurement?
6. Are the proper uses of the Magician's Book and Aslan's Table important to the spiritual life? Why or why not?
7. Aslan tells the children at the end of the story that they were brought to Narnia so that by knowing him a little there, they might get to know him better here. What does this reveal about Lewis' purpose in writing the Narnia tales? How can we get to know Aslan better in our own world?

VI. War against the Powers of Darkness
The Silver Chair

School Stories

Lewis opens *The Silver Chair* by saying it is not going to be a school story. The realistic school story was the most popular form of children's story in the 1950's. Lewis didn't really care for this form of writing for children. He believed that the fairy tale did much more to fortify children to face life.

Comparing the so-called "realistic" children's story to the fairy tale, C. S. Lewis once wrote that what profess to be realistic stories for children are far more likely to deceive them. We don't expect the real world to be like a fairy tale. But some children do expect their school to be like a school story. Therefore fantasies do not deceive as much as the "realistic" stories. All stories where young people do things which seem possible, in the sense that their activities do not break natural law, but where they have successes which are almost infinitely improbable, are in more danger than fairy tales of raising false hopes. Lewis does not suggest that school stories should not be written. He only maintains that school stories are more likely than fairy tales to become 'fantasies' in the psychological sense.

Lewis holds that since it is likely children will meet cruel enemies it is good for them to have heard of brave knights and heroic courage. Otherwise their lives become not brighter but darker. Children need stories with wicked kings and beheadings, battles and dungeons, giants and dragons, with the villains soundly killed at the end. Lewis is persuaded that this does not cause an ordinary child any kind or degree of fear beyond what the child wants or needs to feel. For, of course, says Lewis, every child wants to be a little bit frightened.

According to Lewis, by confining a child to blameless stories of child life in which nothing at all alarming ever happens, we may fail to banish his or her terrors, and we will succeed in removing all that can ennoble them and make life endurable. If a child is going to be frightened, it is better that he or she should think of giants and dragons rather than merely thinking of burglars. St George, or any bright hero clad in armor, is a better comfort than the idea of the police.[230]

Not only did Lewis dislike school stories, he disliked school itself. Experiment House and the bullies who rule the roost there come in for a good trouncing in *The Silver Chair*. Lewis' treatment of this "mixed school", which is not nearly so mixed as the minds of those who run it, is quite humorous. But Lewis' own experience in boarding schools was not at all funny.

C. S. Lewis was first sent off to boarding school at the age of ten, immediately following the death of his mother. As if the trauma of his mother's death, and being sent away from Ireland to England was not enough, Wynyard School in Watford, Hertfordshire was simply abominable. The headmaster, Robert Capron, regularly beat his students with a cane. In the end the school was closed and Capron was later certified insane.[231] The teaching, according to Jack's brother Warnie, who was also a boarder at Wynyard, was at the same time "brutalising and intellectually stupefying".[232]

Lewis' next school, Campbell College, was just around the corner from his home in Belfast. There was bullying at this school, along the lines of Experiment House, though Lewis says no serious share of it came his way.[233] Lewis left Campbell halfway through his first and only term there due to illness. Albert Lewis, dissatisfied with Campbell for some unknown reason, found a new prep school for his younger son in the same town as the college his older son, Warren, was attending: Great Malvern, Worcestershire, England.

---

230 *On Stories*, pp. 37-40. What Lewis says here also seems to agree with what Bruno Bettelheim says on the same subject. See Bettelheim, Bruno, *The Uses of Enchantment: The Meaning and Importance of Fairy Tales*, New York: Random House, 1977, pp. 24, 116-123.
231 Hooper, Walter, *C. S. Lewis: Companion & Guide*, New York: HarperCollins, 1996, pp. 638-640.
232 Sayer, George, *Jack*, p. 59.
233 Lewis, C. S., *Surprised by Joy*, p. 51.

C. S. Lewis went through many important intellectual and spiritual developments at Cherbourg preparatory school and later at Malvern College. But on the whole, he did not enjoy public school life with its compulsory games and fagging system.[234]

A Door to another World

I'm sure Lewis would have loved discovering a door to another world, providing an escape from any one of the public schools he attended. As it was, Lewis' only door to other worlds was through reading great literature. However, the door to Narnia which Eustace and Jill discover at Experiment House is very real to them.

It is interesting to note all the different ways in which children cross over from our world into Narnia. Digory and Polly get to Narnia by use of magic rings. The Pevensies first stumble into Narnia through a wardrobe, and then in *Prince Caspian* they are summoned into Narnia by Susan's magic horn. In *The Horse and His Boy* there is no cross-over from our world to Narnia, or vice versa, because the story takes place wholly in that other world, during the joint reign of High King Peter, Queen Susan, King Edmund and Queen Lucy. In *Voyage of the Dawn Treader* Edmund, Lucy and Eustace enter Narnia through a picture. In *The Silver Chair* Eustace and Jill enter Narnia through a door. And in *The Last Battle*, as we shall see, Eustace and Jill again enter Narnia, but this time they are somehow drawn into Narnia as the result of a railway accident.

The Breath of Aslan

After calling out to Aslan to allow them to go into Narnia, Eustace and Jill discover the door in the wall behind the school gym unlocked. Opening the door they see, not the grey moor and dull autumn sky they expect, but rather sunshine, blue sky and green grass. As they cross through the doorway their classmates' voices behind them suddenly switch off like a radio signal and they find themselves in another world.

---

234 Fagging was a system whereby younger students would perform menial chores for older students, like shining their shoes. For more on Lewis' school life see Will Vaus, *The Professor of Narnia: The C. S. Lewis Story*, Washington, D. C.: Believe Books, 2008.

Before they know it, Eustace and Jill are standing atop a frighteningly high cliff. Jill shows off a bit on the edge and Eustace, trying to pull her back, goes plummeting to the depths. At this point Jill has no time to think of what she has just done, for she realizes a huge lion is beside her somehow blowing Eustace to safety.

This is not the first time we have encountered the miraculous breath of Aslan at work in *The Chronicles of Narnia*. In *The Magician's Nephew* it is the breath of Aslan which imparts the gift of speech to the beasts whom Aslan has chosen. In *The Lion, the Witch and The Wardrobe* it is the breath of Aslan which brings to life the creatures turned to stone by the White Witch. In *The Horse and His Boy* it is the warm breath of Aslan which assures Shasta that Aslan is not a ghost. In *Prince Caspian* it is Aslan's breath which makes Susan brave again and causes a greatness to hang about Edmund. On the *Dawn Treader* it is the voice and sweet breath of Aslan which gives courage to Lucy as the crew tries to escape from the Dark Island.

Nor is this the last time we will feel the breath of Aslan in *The Chronicles*. It is Aslan who will blow Jill to Narnia to join Eustace, and it is the wild breath of Aslan which will blow away Narnia and return the children to Aslan's Mountain at the end of the story. Then in *The Last Battle* it will be the breath of Aslan which takes away Emeth's trembling.

Significantly, the same Greek and Hebrew words in the Bible can be translated either as breath or spirit. In Genesis 2:7 the Lord breathes into the man's nostrils the breath of life and the man becomes a living being. In Job 32:8 it is the breath of the Almighty which gives to human beings their understanding. According to Psalm 33:6, the stars were made by the breath of the Lord's mouth. And in Ezekiel 37:5-6 it is the breath of the Lord which brings to life the valley of dry bones.

Lewis is echoing passages such as these when he speaks about the breath of Aslan. Aslan's breath is his spirit. It is the spirit of Aslan who imparts speech, brings to life, assures and grants courage. It is the spirit of Aslan who sends the children on their rescue mission in search of Prince Rilian, just as it is the Holy Spirit who sends Barnabas and Saul on their mission for Christ.[235]

---

235 See Acts 13:2.

The Stream

After Aslan finishes blowing Eustace to Narnia the Lion walks away into the forest. Jill, being quite thirsty, goes in search of the running water she hears in the distance. Soon she finds an open glade with a stream running through it, but the Lion is also there. The Lion invites her to come and have a drink. His voice makes her frightened in a different way than she was at first; a new kind of fear, or awe, enters her soul. Jill asks the Lion if he won't mind going away while she drinks. His low growl makes her realize what a preposterous request this is. So instead she asks the Lion to promise not to do anything to her. However, the Lion refuses to make such a promise. She asks whether he eats girls and the Lion tells her that he has eaten many people, even cities and entire realms. The Lion tells her that if she doesn't come and drink she will die of thirst. Jill responds by saying that she must then go look for another stream. But there is no other stream, says Aslan. Thus Jill bends down by the stream to drink, even though it is the hardest thing she has ever done.

This encounter between Aslan and Jill is reminiscent of Jesus' encounter with the woman at the well. Jesus says to her,

> If you knew the gift of God and who it is that asks you for a drink, you would have asked him and he would have given you living water.[236]

Jesus says the water he gives will become a spring of water welling up to eternal life.[237]

When Aslan tells Jill that there is no other stream it reminds us of Jesus' statement: "I am the way and the truth and the life. No one comes to the Father except through me."[238]

Jill's desire to find another stream is like the attempt of the Jews in the Old Testament to forsake the Lord, the spring of living water, and dig out their own cisterns, broken cisterns which cannot hold water.[239]

---

236 John 4:10.
237 John 4:14.
238 John 14:6. See also Acts 4:12.
239 See Jeremiah 2:13.

Calling

After Jill has quenched her thirst at the stream, the Lion tells her he has a task for her and Eustace. In fact, this task is the reason why Aslan has called Jill and Eustace out of their own world. Jill thinks the Lion must be confusing her with someone else, because it was she and Eustace who asked to come into Narnia; it was not they who were called but they who called. At this point Aslan tells Jill that she would not have called to him unless he had been calling her.[240]

This reminds us of the Scriptural teaching that it is God's call upon our lives which enables us to call out to him. Jesus said,

> All that the Father gives me will come to me, and whoever comes to me I will never drive away. . . . No one can come to me unless the Father who sent me draws him, and I will raise him up at the last day.[241]

Remember the Signs

Aslan assigns to Jill and Eustace the task of finding and rescuing lost Prince Rilian. This task is similar to the task of Christian evangelism – finding lost people, people who are under an enchantment and have forgotten their true identity, and then bringing them home to the Father's house.[242]

When Jill asks Aslan how they are to find the lost Prince, Aslan proceeds to give her four signs to follow. Jill doesn't know what to say in response, so she thanks Aslan and tells him that she sees. But Aslan tells her she doesn't really see as well as she thinks, and that the most important thing is to remember the signs. Aslan has Jill repeat the signs until she has them fully memorized. Before Aslan blows Jill to Narnia he urges her to say the signs to herself every morning, every night, and even in the middle of the night. Then he warns her that everything which seems clear to her on the mountain top will not be so obvious when she drops down into the thick air of Narnia. The signs which she has learned may not look at all as she expects. Jill is to pay no attention to appearances, but rather she is to remember the signs and believe them.

---

240 Lewis, C. S., *The Silver Chair*, New York: Macmillan, 1973, p. 19.
241 John 6:37, 44.
242 See Luke 15.

Aslan's command to remember the signs is an allusion to Moses' entreaty to the Israelites:

> These commandments that I give you today are to be upon your hearts. Impress them on your children. Talk about them when you sit at home and when you walk along the road, when you lie down and when you get up.[243]

The Christian is to remember God's word in the Bible, believe it and follow it, even when it may not make sense in the thick air of our world. We are not to pay attention to appearances, but rather, do what God says–no matter what.

Jill's movement from mountaintop to valley, from clarity to confusion, is reminiscent of Moses coming down from Mount Sinai with the Ten Commandments, only to find the Israelites worshiping a golden calf.[244] Or we might think of Peter, James and John overcome by their awesome experience on the mountain with Jesus, Moses and Elijah, and then having to descend and face a demon-possessed boy.[245]

For Jill, Aslan's warning is all too prophetic. As soon as Jill arrives in Narnia and meets up with Scrubb she forgets the signs for at least a half hour[246] and the children end up missing Eustace's old and dear friend, King Caspian, who could have provided them with help. After meeting the Lady of the Green Kirtle, Jill altogether gives up her habit of repeating the signs to herself. This failure on Jill's part causes her and Puddleglum and Eustace to miss, at first, the ruins of the giant city and the writing on the stones.

Appearances of Evil

Aslan's other warning to Jill, to pay no attention to appearances, also becomes very important in the ensuing adventure. The Lady of the Green Kirtle *appears* to be very kind and helpful to the children. Eustace thinks she is "super" and Jill is quite impressed by her dress and her horse. Trusting to appearances, the children buy into the Lady's lie that the giants at Harfang are more gentle, mild, civil, prudent and

---

243 Deuteronomy 6:6-7.
244 See Exodus 32.
245 See Mark 9:2-29.
246 *The Silver Chair*, p. 29.

courteous than the giants of Ettinsmoor. The Lady of the Green Kirtle baits the children with the promise of steaming baths, soft beds, and delicious meals at Harfang, and the children take the bait.

We learn from the Parliament of Owls[247] that a woman wrapped in a green garment baited Rilian with her beauty. But this same beautiful woman also turned into a hideous green serpent, a venomous worm that killed Rilian's mother. Amazingly, Jill is able to recognize from the owl's story that the woman and the serpent are the same person. Yet Jill doesn't recognize the Lady of the Green Kirtle as being the one who killed Rilian's mother and captured Rilian himself. The problem, of course, is that Jill and Eustace are putting their trust in appearances rather than following Aslan's signs.

In Scripture we are told that Satan himself masquerades as an angel of light. Therefore we should not be surprised when Satan's servants masquerade as servants of righteousness.[248] We need to always be on our guard against enchantments just as Puddleglum warns the children,[249] for the devil prowls around like a roaring lion looking for people to devour.[250] And when we do encounter Satan, the serpent, we must respond as Jesus did in the wilderness,[251] we must stick to the signs and use Scripture as our one offensive weapon against Satan's wiles.[252]

Aslan's Providence

Though the enchantments of evil prove powerful in *The Silver Chair* the providence of Aslan is more powerful still. Aslan not only provides the signs for Jill to follow, but we may assume that Aslan is orchestrating other things behind the scenes. Are the arrival of Glimfeather the Owl and the provision of Puddleglum the Marsh-wiggle mere accidents? Not in Aslan's world. And Aslan even points out the ruined city and the message thereon to Jill, in a dream, *after* she has failed to follow his signs on her own.

---

247 The name, *Parliament of Owls*, is based upon the title of a poem by Geoffrey Chaucer: *The Parliament of Fowles*.
248 See 2 Corinthians 11:14-15.
249 *The Silver Chair*, p. 73.
250 1 Peter 5:8-9.
251 See Matthew 4:1-11.
252 See Ephesians 6:17.

Eustace expresses faith in Aslan's providence when he says he doesn't think Aslan would ever have sent them on their mission if there was little chance of success.[253] But in the end, it is Puddleglum himself who shows the deepest faith in Aslan.

Puddleglum displays unshakable trust in Aslan's guidance when he maintains vociferously that Aslan's instructions always work, without exception.[254] Puddleglum even finds encouragement in the darkness of Underworld because at least they are back on the right track, following Aslan's directions.[255] And one of Puddleglum's most ringing statements of faith is made in the teeth of Rilian's denial of the meaning of the writing in the ancient giant city. Puddleglum affirms that there are no accidents and that Aslan is their guide. Aslan was there when the giant king caused the letters to be cut in the giant city, and Aslan knew already all things that would come of the king's action, including their discovery of the words.[256]

Lewis says something similar about God's providence in his book *Miracles*. He affirms that if God directs the course of all events in the universe then God certainly directs the movement of every atom every minute.[257] Lewis quotes Jesus' saying as authority for his belief: "Are not two sparrows sold for a penny? Yet not one of them will fall to the ground apart from the will of your Father."[258]

What is Reality?

The biggest question raised in *The Silver Chair* is: What is reality? Prince Rilian has forgotten reality. He does not know that he is Prince Rilian. He does not remember having lived anywhere else but the Dark World. He thinks the Lady of the Green Kirtle, the Queen of Underland, is a fountain of all virtues, and that she has saved him from some evil enchantment, whereas she has, in reality, bound him in the chains of darkness.

---

253 *The Silver Chair*, p.64.
254 Ibid. p. 104.
255 Ibid. p. 128.
256 Ibid. p. 134.
257 *Miracles*, p. 174.
258 Matthew 10:29

Rilian, while he is bound by the Green Witch's enchantment, thinks the hour he spends in the silver chair every night is the hour of his madness, when in reality it is the one hour when he is sane. Even the children and Puddleglum don't know what to think when Rilian, in the silver chair, begs them to loose him from his bonds. That is, they don't know what to think or do until Rilian implores them *in the name of Aslan*. The mention of the name of Aslan makes everything plain, for it is the fourth sign which Aslan gave Jill on the mountain top. Puddleglum leads the children in freeing Rilian from the silver chair and from his enchantment, despite the possible danger which may come to them, for Aslan didn't tell them what would happen, he only told them what to do.

Though following Aslan's instructions frees Rilian from his enchantment, it does not mark the end of everyone's battle against the powers of darkness. The Queen of Underland soon reappears and seeks to enslave not only Rilian, but Puddleglum, Eustace and Jill as well, using, in part, physical means. She enchants them using a green powder which works like incense when it is thrown on the fire. She also seduces them through strumming on a mandolin.

However, the Queen's enchantment is not merely wrought by physical means she also seeks to enslave them by intellectual means. In fact, the two methods are intertwined. The more the sickly sweet smell of the incense hangs in the air, and the longer the Queen strums on her mandolin, the harder it is for the Prince and the others to think clearly. The Queen tells them there is no land of Narnia, in fact, she says, there is no Overworld at all. She suggests that the things they have dreamt of in their play-land called Overworld are merely based upon things they have really known in her world. In essence the Queen questions everyone's knowledge of objective reality and maintains that what they *think* is objective reality is merely a subjective dream.

It has been said that in Lewis' pattern of thinking there is no indication of the questions being thrown up by postmodernism today. But one of the things maintained by postmodernism is that there is no objective reality – and this is the very question Lewis deals with in *The Silver Chair*. And not only does Lewis deal with the question here, but also in his essay, *The Poison of Subjectivism*, as well as in his book, *The*

Abolition of Man. In the former Lewis maintains that unless we return to a crude and nursery-like belief in objective value, humanity itself will perish.[259] Lewis foresaw the coming of postmodernism back in the 1940's in Oxford. He knew there would come a time when some people would no longer submit to reasoned arguments for the Christian faith or for objective values. That is one reason why he wrote *The Chronicles of Narnia*, so that he might steal past watchful dragons and baptize the imaginations of those who would no longer allow reason to guide them to the truth.

The Green Witch's line of questioning aims at a sort of undermining of belief in supernatural reality. According to the witch there is nothing above them, there is no Overworld. There is only the dark world in which they are now living. What the witch is recommending is pure naturalism, mere materialism; believe in what you can touch, taste, feel, see and smell around you–nothing else.

Breaking the Spell

How is the twin spell of naturalism and subjectivism to be undone? In *The Silver Chair* this twin spell is broken by two acts on the part of Puddleglum. First, he stamps out the witch's fire with the incense burning on it. The smell of burnt Marsh-wiggle temporarily clears everyone's head. Physical forms of temptation are met by physical resistance. The pain in Puddleglum's foot also clears his brain and he answers the witch with an argument which runs as follows: So what if there is no Narnia and no Aslan? Our play world licks your real world any day. And how, after all, could we dream up a play world that is better than the real one? After Puddleglum's statement, the mental battle turns purely physical as the witch is transformed into a giant serpent and Prince Rilian does battle with her, killing her with his sword.

C. S. Lewis did much through his writing and speaking to try to break the enchantments of naturalism and subjectivism which he believed were upon many people around him. He asks his listeners in his sermon, *The Weight of Glory* whether they think he is trying to weave a spell. He admits that perhaps he is. But he urges his

259 Lewis, C. S., *Christian Reflections*, London: Geoffrey Bles, 1967, p. 81.

hearers to remember their fairy tales. Spells can be used for breaking enchantments as well as for inducing them. Lewis holds that we are in need of the strongest spell possible to free us from the evil enchantment of worldliness which has been laid upon the world for the past hundred years or more.[260]

Cosmic Results

Once Rilian's enchantment is broken and the Queen of Underland is killed, the children and Puddleglum and the Prince slowly come to realize that their actions have had cosmic results. The first thing they hear is that the once quiet Earthmen are celebrating outside the witch's castle. Then they recognize an earthquake is taking place. Their first assumption is that the earthquake and the consequent fires and floods are a result of a chain of magic spells the Queen of Underland put in place to take effect upon her death. But later, after their conversation with one of the Earthmen named Golg, Prince Rilian and the others come to understand that by their actions they have freed the Earthmen who had been enslaved to the Green Witch.

In a similar fashion Scripture teaches us that Jesus bound Satan during his earthly ministry[261] and dealt the death blow to Satan upon the cross.[262] This mortal blow to the serpent is foretold in Genesis 3:15, "he will crush your head, and you will strike his heal." Furthermore, by his ascension to heaven Jesus took captive all the demon hosts.[263] Jesus' life, death, resurrection and ascension are bringing about cosmic results for good. Certainly some of these results are not fully evident yet, but the full redemption of creation is on its way.[264] Jesus is *the* Prince of Peace who has conquered the powers of darkness and will bring his victory to completion.

---

260 *The Weight of Glory*, p. 7.
261 See Mark 3:20-30 and Revelation 20:1-3.
262 Notice, according to one of the evangelists, an earthquake immediately followed the death of Christ on the cross, thus declaring the cosmic implications of his sacrificial death. See Matthew 27:51.
263 Ephesians 4:8.
264 See Romans 8:18-25.

On Aslan's Mountain

When Eustace and Jill return to Cair Paravel after rescuing Prince Rilian they witness the death of King Caspian. It is at this moment that the children hear a golden voice behind them; they turn and see Aslan, and as Jill sees the Lion all she can think of is her mistakes. Like Isaiah in the presence of the Lord, she is undone by her sin in the presence of Aslan's holiness.[265] But immediately the Lion tells her to think no more of such things, for he will not always be scolding, just as the Lord says in Isaiah 57:16,

> I will not accuse forever,
> nor will I always be angry,
> for then the spirit of man would grow faint before me–
> the breath of man that I have created.

Suddenly Aslan blows away the reality of Cair Paravel; Eustace and Jill find themselves atop Aslan's Mountain again. The strange thing is that the funeral music for King Caspian is still ringing in their ears, and as they look into Aslan's stream, there they see the dead king himself. All three stand there weeping, even Aslan, for "precious in the sight of the Lord is the death of his saints."[266]

Then Aslan asks Eustace to go and pluck a thorn from the thicket and drive it into his paw. The thorn is a foot long and very sharp. Eustace obeys and drives the thorn into the pad of Aslan's paw. The blood trickles out into the stream and over the dead body of the king. At this moment the funeral music stops and the dead king begins to change. His hair turns from grey to blonde, his body grows younger and suddenly he leaps up laughing and alive before them. The new Caspian embraces Aslan and greets the children with astonishment. The children are hesitant at first, thinking Caspian is a ghost, but he assures them he is not.

Here we have a foreshadowing of the great resurrection which will take place at the end of Narnia, at the end of *The Last Battle*. It is a resurrection accomplished by the blood of Aslan. For now, Caspian awakes into a world where he cannot want wrong things anymore.

---

265 See Isaiah 6:1-5.
266 See Psalm 116:15.

If *The Chronicles of Narnia* teach us anything, they teach that the war against the powers of darkness is ongoing. At the end of *The Lion, the Witch and the Wardrobe* it seems the conclusion to the story is that the people of Narnia lived happily ever after. But then in *Prince Caspian* there is the war with Miraz. And now again in *The Silver Chair* there is another war with a witch who is very much like the White Witch. Will the war against the powers of darkness ever end? For an answer to that question we must turn to *The Last Battle*. But in the meantime we are left with the good news that Caspian's war with darkness *has* come to an end and he is beginning a new and wonderful life on Aslan's Mountain.

Discussion Questions

1. What do you think of Lewis' attitude toward school as expressed in *The Silver Chair*?
2. What spiritual truths impacted you from reading about Jill's encounter with Aslan on the mountain?
3. How can we best "remember the signs" in our own world and carry out Aslan's mission?
4. How do you feel about Puddleglum? What are his vices and virtues?
5. What do you think of the Lady of the Green Kirtle as a personification of evil? In what ways is she the same as the White Witch and the Queen of Charn? How is she different?
6. What does this story have to teach us about spiritual warfare?
7. How does this story address the issues of postmodernism, particularly, lack of belief in objective values and absolute truth?

VII. The Coming of the Antichrist, the End of the World, and the Last Judgment

The Last Battle

In the opening chapter of *The Last Battle* Lewis shows us how a great evil can begin in a small and seemingly innocent manner, thus suggesting that apparently little sins should be nipped in the bud. The very first characters to which we are introduced at the beginning of *The Last Battle* are Shift the ape and Puzzle the donkey. Shift is a very clever, manipulating, self-centered animal, whereas Puzzle is not so clever, rather malleable, but on the whole more righteous than the ape. The whole undoing of Narnia starts with the ape's discovery of a lion skin in Caldron Pool. Shift's idea is to put the lion skin on Puzzle and trick the other Narnians into thinking that Puzzle is really Aslan so that Shift can get whatever he wants out of them. Puzzle realizes this is a bad idea, but he gives in to Shift nonetheless. Thus Puzzle has a conscience, whereas Shift has nothing but his own greed.

In his 1961 letter to Anne Waller Jenkins, Lewis indicates that Shift the ape is like the antichrist in our world. The word *antichrist*, meaning the one who is against the Messiah, is used only four times in the Bible, exclusively in the Johannine letters. In those letters we are told that *the* antichrist is coming, but also that *many* antichrists have already come.[267] Who are these antichrists? Anyone who denies that Jesus is the Christ, such a person is an antichrist; such a person is denying the Father/Son relationship between God and Jesus.[268] Every spirit who does not acknowledge Jesus is not from God. This is the spirit of the antichrist.[269] Anyone who does not acknowledge Jesus as coming in the flesh, as fully human, such a person is a deceiver and an antichrist.[270]

---

267 1 John 2:18.
268 1 John 2:22.
269 1 John 4:3.
270 2 John 1:7.

Jesus himself warned his disciples that many would come in his name claiming, "I am he," and deceive many.[271] And the Apostle Paul said that before Jesus' return a great rebellion would occur and "the lawless one" would be revealed. The coming of this lawless one will be in accordance with the work of Satan, and will be displayed in counterfeit miracles.[272] Furthermore, the book of Revelation talks about a beast to whom will be given the authority of Satan,[273] and a false prophet associated with the beast.[274] In the end, these two, along with Satan, will be thrown into a fiery lake of burning sulfur.[275]

In *The Last Battle* Lewis is certainly drawing on biblical imagery to develop his picture of the ape and the donkey and their relationship. Shift is a type of antichrist in that he denies, by his actions, the reality of Aslan. Puzzle, in dressing up like Aslan, is like the beast of Revelation who pretends to be the Christ, and Shift is like the false prophet. Shift, in the end, is devoured by the demon Tash, just as the false prophet is destroyed in a lake of burning fire. However, Lewis changes the portrait in the book of Revelation, in that Puzzle is merely a pawn of Shift, and in the end Puzzle is saved, rather than destroyed by Aslan. Furthermore, Shift is not the only evil character in this story. In fact, the dominant evil role is taken away from Shift, toward the end of the story, and given to Rishda Tarkaan and Ginger the cat.

Not a Tame Lion

When the ape first begins to carry out his plans, and Puzzle dresses up as Aslan, there is some confusion in the minds of the Narnians as to what is really going on. King Tirian and Jewel the unicorn hear tales of the arrival of Aslan in Narnia; but can it be true? Roonwit the centaur thinks not, for the stars tell a different tale, a tale of terrible doings. Jewel suggests that Aslan may have come to Narnia even though the stars say otherwise, for Aslan is not a tame lion; he is not the slave of stars but rather their creator.

When Tirian and Jewel are told that Talking Trees are being felled in Lantern Waste by Aslan's orders, they wonder again: Could this

---

271 Mark 13:5.
272 2 Thessalonians 2:1-12.
273 Revelation 13
274 Revelation 16:13.
275 Revelation 19:20; 20:10

really be Aslan's doing? Once again Jewel remarks that Aslan is *not a tame lion*.

Shift uses the phrase – "not a tame lion" – to mean all sorts of horrible things. The ape tells the Narnian beasts that Aslan is going to whip them into shape; he isn't going to be soft anymore. Aslan will teach them to think he is a tame lion.[276]

Of course, the idea of Aslan not being a tame lion goes all the way back to *The Lion, the Witch and the Wardrobe*. The original truth conveyed there is that Aslan is wild and, in a sense, unpredictable. He can't be tied down.[277] However, in *The Last Battle* the use of this phrase – "not a tame lion" – raises the question: Would Aslan command something seemingly evil, and does Aslan's command make something automatically good? Lewis' answer to this question is a definite: No!

Lewis deals with the whole issue of God's goodness in *The Problem of Pain*. In that book he says that if God's goodness differs from our conception of goodness as black differs from white, then we can mean nothing by calling God good. Lewis goes on to assert that certainly God's goodness *is* different from ours, but God's goodness does not differ from our goodness as black from white. Rather it is like a perfect circle compared to a child's attempt at drawing a circle. When the child has learned to draw he will realize that the perfect circle is the one he was trying to make all along.[278]

Taking the Adventure Aslan Sends

Though the presence of evil throughout *The Last Battle* brings with it a sense of confusion, the good characters in this story are determined to go on and take the adventure which Aslan sends to them. This phrase, *taking the adventure Aslan sends*, carries with it a strong sense of Aslan's sovereignty. Though Aslan never appears in Old Narnia in *The Last Battle*, Tirian, Jewel and the others trust Aslan nevertheless. Tirian and Jewel stride forth confidently to handle whatever may be happening at

---

276 Lewis, C. S., *The Last Battle,* New York: Macmillan, 1973, p. 28.
277 See *The Lion, the Witch and the Wardrobe*, p. 180.
278 *The Problem of Pain*, pp. 37-39.

Lantern Waste at the beginning of the story.[279] They march forth no less assuredly to declare the truth on Stable Hill toward the end of the book. They are able to do this because they trust that Aslan is really in charge despite all appearances to the contrary.[280] Even as they hide behind the stable, within a hair's breadth of all the concentrated evil in Narnia, Tirian assures Jill that they are between the paws of the true Aslan, whatever tribulation they may have to face.[281]

Tashlan

The confusion of good and evil only gets greater when the ape tells the Narnian beasts that Tash is only another name for Aslan. Tash is the god of the Calormenes, a beast with four arms and the head of a vulture on whose altar people are sacrificed. The ape tells the Narnians that the old idea of the Calormenes being wrong and the Narnians being right is ridiculous. The difference is merely one of semantics—the Calormenes use different words but mean the same thing. Tirian longs to ask the ape how Tash, who is fed on the blood of his people, could be the same as Aslan, who gave his blood for the salvation of Narnia. However, Tirian never gets the chance to ask his question. Eventually the ape and his followers start calling their new god Tashlan, but some, like Ginger the cat and Rishda Tarkaan, don't believe in the reality of either Tash or Aslan. Fittingly, Tash, who is really a demon,[282] does show up in the end, frightening Ginger into imbecility, capturing Rishda Tarkaan and gobbling up the ape.

Jesus warned against this kind of confusion of good with evil. When the teachers of the law said that Jesus cast out demons by the power of the prince of demons, Jesus responded by saying:

> How can Satan drive out Satan? If a kingdom is divided against itself, that kingdom cannot stand. If a house is divided against itself, that house cannot stand. And if Satan opposes himself and is divided, he cannot stand; his end has come. In fact, no one can enter a strong man's house and carry off his possessions unless he first ties up the strong man. Then he can

---
279 *The Last Battle*, p. 20.
280 Ibid. pp. 92, 94.
281 Ibid. p. 107.
282 Ibid. p. 83.

rob his house. I tell you the truth, all the sins and blasphemies of men will be forgiven them. But whoever blasphemes against the Holy Spirit will never be forgiven; he is guilty of an eternal sin.

The Gospel of Mark adds the comment that Jesus said this because the teachers of the law were saying he had an evil spirit.[283]

The confusion of evil with good, and the claim that all religions are really the same, is something we must watch out for in our own world. In *Mere Christianity* Lewis contends that Christians are free to believe that all religions contain at least a hint of the truth. However, being a Christian means thinking that where Christianity differs from other religions Christianity is right and the other religions are wrong. Lewis compares the situation to arithmetic where there is only one right answer to a problem but some of the wrong answers are closer to being right than others.[284]

The Last Battle

Of course the height of the action in this story comes with the last battle in Old Narnia which Lewis describes splendidly. One wonders whether Lewis' fine ability to paint the picture of battle scenes comes more from his own experiences in World War I or from his reading of medieval literature, or both. Certainly all the Narnian battles are medieval in character, using bows and arrows, swords and daggers, rather than guns and tanks, and airplanes and bombs. However, only someone who had experienced warfare could describe the feeling of being in the middle of a battle as well as Lewis does.

When the ape and his crew set out to throw the Narnians into the stable to meet their death, Tirian and Jewel take their stand, along with their helpers from our world, Jill and Eustace. Tirian calls all true Narnians to his side, while Rishda Tarkaan makes his counter-claim on the Narnians' loyalty, threatening the wrath of Tashlan. The first thing Tirian does is to throw the ape into the stable where he is eaten up by Tash. However, Rishda too has his plans to use the stable. He orders his men to drive Tirian and his army into the stable so the Calormenes

---

283 See Mark 3:20-30.
284 *Mere Christianity*, p. 43.

can set fire to it. The true Narnians win the first skirmish, but before they know it, the Dwarfs are fighting against them as well, and the Calormenes beat their drums to call for reinforcements. Though the Narnians fight on valiantly, they are eventually outnumbered by the Calormene army. Before long, Eustace and Jill, and finally Tirian, are thrown into the stable, though Tirian takes Rishda Tarkaan with him.

In contrast to Lewis who takes a chapter and a half to describe the last battle of Narnia, the author of Revelation takes only eleven verses in one place and four in another to describe the final conflict between good and evil in our world.[285] The place of "the last battle" in the Bible is called Armageddon and it is the spirits of demons who call the kings of the whole world to gather them for war.[286] The name *Armageddon* is given to the place of the final war between good and evil in our world because the plain of Megiddo in Palestine was the location for many ancient battles.[287]

One thing which may be surprising to some readers of *The Last Battle* is that Aslan never comes to fight, in person, with the Narnians at all. There is no "second coming" of Aslan to Narnia as the Bible indicates there is to be a second coming of Christ to our world. In Revelation it is Christ himself who comes to vanquish the beast and the false prophet.[288] Not so in Narnia. Aslan leaves Tirian and the true Narnians to fight the battle themselves. And rather than having the New Jerusalem come down to earth from heaven[289] Lewis has the Old Narnians drawn into the New Narnia through the stable door.

---

285 See Revelation 19:11-21; 20:7-10.
286 Revelation 16:14, 16.
287 On the plains of Megiddo Pharaoh Thutmose III defeated a Canaanite coalition in 1468 B. C. Deborah and Barak crushed the Canaanites by the waters of Megiddo (Judges 5:19). Good King Josiah died in battle here against Pharaoh Neco II in 609 B. C. (2 Kings 23:29; 2 Chronicles 35:22). And more recently, the British under General Allenby ended the rule of the Turks in Palestine by conquering them in the Valley of Jezreel opposite Megiddo in 1917.
288 See again Revelation 19:11-21.
289 See Revelation 21:1-3.

On the Other Side of the Stable Door

After seizing Rishda and drawing him into the stable with him, the first thing Tirian realizes is that he is not in a dark stable at all, but rather he is standing in the blinding light of day. Rishda is wailing and pointing. Tirian, following Rishda's pointing finger, sees Tash coming and swooping Rishda up under his arm. Then Tirian hears a strong and calm voice telling Tash to be gone with his lawful prey. He turns to see who has spoken and sees, standing before him, seven kings and queens, richly attired, and when he looks at his own clothes he is amazed to find that he is similarly arrayed. The seven kings and queens are, in order: Digory, Polly, Peter, Edmund, Lucy, Eustace and Jill.

Rather than standing in a tiny hovel of a stable Tirian realizes he is standing on green grass, with blue sky overhead and with a sweet breeze blowing in his face. Not far away there is an orchard with glowing fruits. This fruit corresponds to the fruit of the tree of life in the book of Revelation.[290] At first, Tirian and his new friends are not sure they are meant to eat the fruits, but then they conclude that they have come to a country where everything is allowed and no one can desire anything bad. As they are eating the fruit of the trees the friends begin to talk about how they came to this beautiful land. Edmund, Peter and Digory begin to describe the events at the railway station, how there was a loud roar and something hitting them with a bang, followed by feelings of lightness, total health, and in the case of the oldsters, Digory and Polly, un-stiffening.

Beside this group of people there is the stable door, free standing with no walls attached to it. When Tirian puts his eye to a crack in the door he can see the bonfire amidst the darkness of Lantern Waste. Tirian comments how the stable within and the stable seen from without are two different places. A stable bigger inside than outside, adds Digory. Then Lucy offers the deepest insight when she says that in our world there was once a stable which had something inside it bigger than our whole world; of course she is referring to the stable in which Jesus was born.

---

290 See Revelation 22:2.

The Absence of Susan

Some readers of *The Last Battle* have been troubled by the absence of Susan in the new Narnia. When Tirian asks about this, King Peter explains that Susan is no longer a friend of Narnia. Eustace adds that Susan now treats Narnia like it is make-believe. Jill comments that Susan is interested in nothing now but nylons, lipstick and invitations to parties. Some readers have thought that Lewis had a problem with Susan growing up and being interested in the things that many teenage girls normally focus upon. But Polly suggests Susan's problem is that she refuses to *keep* growing. According to Polly, Susan wasted her childhood wanting to be a teenager and she will waste the rest of her life trying to *remain* a teenager.

At least one reader who was bothered about Susan's absence in the last of the Narnia tales wrote to Lewis about it. Here is Lewis' comment on the matter:

> The books don't tell us what happened to Susan. She is left alive in this world at the end, having by then turned into a rather silly, conceited young woman. But there is plenty of time for her to mend, and perhaps she will get to Aslan's country in the end – in her own way. I think that whatever she had seen in Narnia she *could* (if she was the sort that wanted to) persuade herself, as she grew up, that it was "all nonsense". [291]

The Coming of Aslan & the Dwarfs' Predicament

After telling the tale of the people they had seen come through the stable door Lucy invites Tirian to come and see the dwarfs and perhaps help them if he can. The curious thing about these old Narnian dwarfs is that they are all huddled in a circle, convinced they are in the darkness of the stable. Lucy tries to alter the dwarfs' thinking by holding a bunch of flowers up to one of their noses, but the dwarf is sure it is only stable litter. Tirian attempts to awaken the same dwarf, Diggle by name, to his real surroundings, by swinging him out of the circle of his friends. However, Diggle complains that Tirian has smashed his face against the stable wall, and he trundles back to his fellow dwarfs.

---

291 *Letters to Children* [22 January 1957], p. 67.

Suddenly Aslan is in their midst and the first thing he does is to commend Tirian saying: Well done! Aslan saying "Well done!" echoes Jesus' Parable about the Talents. In that parable the master of the house returns after a long journey to settle accounts with his servants and commends the servant who has well employed his talents saying:

> Well done, good and faithful servant! You have been faithful with a few things; I will put you in charge of many things. Come and share your master's happiness.[292]

After this interlude Lucy asks Aslan to help the dwarfs, if he can. Aslan tells Lucy he will show her what he can and cannot do. Aslan roars, but the dwarfs think it is some kind of machine. The Lion provides the dwarfs with a glorious feast, but they think it is made of the things one might commonly find in a stable. Even so the dwarfs end up arguing over their scraps. Aslan concludes by saying that the dwarfs will not let him help them. They have chosen cunning instead of faith. The dwarfs' prison is only in their own minds, but they are so afraid of being taken in that they cannot be taken out of that prison.

This incident reminds us of what Lewis says elsewhere about hell. In *The Great Divorce* Lewis' character, George MacDonald, says that hell is indeed a state of mind. Every state of mind, left to itself, every shutting up of a creature within the dungeon of its own mind – is, in the end, hell.[293]

The End of Old Narnia & the Final Judgment

Aslan himself is the one who brings Old Narnia to an end as he stands at the stable door and calls for Father Time to do his work. The great giant Time raises a horn to his mouth and blows. Immediately the sky is full of shooting stars. This mirrors the prophecy of Isaiah:

> All the stars of the heavens will be dissolved
> and the sky rolled up like a scroll;
> all the starry host will fall
> like withered leaves from the vine,
> like shriveled figs from the fig tree.[294]

---

292 See Matthew 25:14-30 and Luke 19:11-27.
293 *The Great Divorce*, p. 63.
294 Isaiah 34:4. See also Isaiah 13:10 and Matthew 24:29.

However, the Narnian stars are really people, and so these glittering people rush down toward Tirian and his friends out of the black air and come to stand behind them. Their light allows Tirian and the other kings and queens to see what happens next.

What does happen next is that all the creatures and people of Narnia come to the stable door and face Aslan. All of them must look straight into Aslan's face. Some look into the face of Aslan with fear and hatred and then disappear into the shadow at Aslan's left. Others look into the lion's face and love him, entering the New Narnia at Aslan's right.

The final judgment of Narnia dovetails with what Jesus said about the final judgment of our world in his Parable of the Sheep and the Goats. In the parable, the Son of Man separates the sheep from the goats, placing the sheep on his right and the goats on his left. The King invites the sheep to take the kingdom prepared for them since the creation of the world, but he tells the goats to depart from him into the eternal fire prepared for the devil and his angels. The judgment is based upon the sheep and goats' treatment of the brothers and sisters of the Son of Man.[295]

The last judgment of Narnia, however, is based solely on the creature's response to Aslan. Those who hate him disappear into nothingness; those who love him enter in to never-ending blessedness. This reminds us of what Jesus said about people's reaction in our world to the Son of God:

> For God so loved the world that he gave his one and only Son, that whoever believes in him shall not perish but have eternal life. For God did not send his Son into the world to condemn the world, but to save the world through him. Whoever believes in him is not condemned, but whoever does not believe stands condemned already because he has not believed in the name of God's one and only Son. This is the verdict: Light has come into the world, but men loved darkness instead of light because their deeds were evil. Everyone who does evil hates the light, and will not come into the light for fear that his deeds will be exposed. But whoever lives by the truth comes into the light,

---

295 See Matthew 25:31-46.

so that it may be seen plainly that what he has done has been done through God.²⁹⁶

After the final judgment of Narnia the great dragons and giant lizards start chewing up all the vegetation of the Old Narnia until the whole world is only bare rock and earth. This is similar to what Peter says in 2 Peter 3:10 about the earth and everything in it being laid bare in the end.

The very end of Narnia echoes the prophecy of Joel where the Scripture talks about the sun being turned to darkness and the moon to blood before the coming of the day of the Lord.²⁹⁷ When the sun rises the last time in old Narnia it is a large red sun, similar to the one Digory and Polly saw in Charn during its last days. In the reflection of the sun the sea looks like blood and the moon also looks red. The sun shoots out flames and draws the moon to itself; as the two are joined together, great lumps of fire drop out of this flaming ball into the ocean. Finally, at the word of Aslan, Father Time puts an end to Narnia by reaching out and grabbing the sun, squeezing it like an orange until there is total darkness. And Aslan has the High King Peter shut the stable door on Old Narnia, scraping over the ice as it closes.

Emeth

After closing the door on Old Narnia, Aslan invites the kings and queens to follow him further in and further up into his own new country. The kings and queens cannot keep up with Aslan; meanwhile they come upon the former Calormene soldier named Emeth,²⁹⁸ the one who entered the stable door because he wanted to meet Tash face to face.

Emeth tells the kings and queens about his encounter with Aslan in this new land. To his own astonishment, Emeth is welcomed by Aslan even though he protests that he has been a servant of Tash. Aslan tells Emeth the service he has given to Tash has been accounted as service to him. So Emeth queries whether Tash and Aslan are the same.

---

296 John 3:16-21.
297 See Joel 2:30-31 and also Acts 2:19-20 and 2 Peter 3:7, 12.
298 Interestingly enough, *emeth* is the word for truth in Hebrew. Emeth is certainly a seeker of truth.

The Lion growls and tells Emeth this is a falsehood. In fact, Aslan and Tash are opposites. Aslan accepts Emeth's good deeds done in the name of Tash as done to Aslan himself because no good service can be done to Tash and no evil service can truly be done in the name of Aslan. Furthermore, Aslan assures Emeth that he would not have sought so long and so truly unless his desire had been for him.

Many people question whether Lewis is teaching some sort of universalism here. Is Lewis saying that all people will be saved no matter what religion they follow, so long as they follow sincerely? No, I don't think so. Rather, Emeth is the working out, in story form, of certain ideas Lewis talks about elsewhere, biblical ideas in fact.

Returning to Jesus' Parable of the Sheep and the Goats we can see that the sheep have served the King, the Son of Man, without knowing it.[299] Lewis rightly points out that this parable is about the judgment of the nations; it is about the judgment of people who have not known Israel's God. The parable indeed suggests that some people will find eternal salvation because they have served the one true God without knowing it. Just so, Emeth has served Aslan without knowing him.

Lewis makes the same point in a letter written on 8 November 1952. In that letter he suggests that every prayer sincerely made, even to a false god or to a very imperfectly conceived true God, is accepted by the true God. Christ saves many who do not think they know him, because Christ is, however dimly, present in the *good* side of the inferior teachers whom some people follow.[300]

Lewis maintains that those who have heard of Christ in our world need to come to him through faith in order to find eternal salvation. However, Lewis holds out hope that even those who haven't heard of Christ may be saved by his grace. As he writes in *Mere Christianity*, God has not told us what his arrangements will be for those who have not heard of Christ. Lewis asserts that Christ is the only way of salvation. However, he maintains, we don't know that *only* those who have *heard* of Christ in this life will be saved through him.[301]

---

299 See Matthew 25:37-39.
300 *Letters*, p. 428.
301 *Mere Christianity*, p. 65. Lewis also held out hope of eternal salvation for those, like his adopted mother Janie King Moore, who seemingly rejected Christ in

The New Narnia

As the kings and queens journey on after their meeting with Emeth they try to figure out exactly where they are. This new land reminds them in some ways of Narnia. Finally the truth begins to dawn on them. Digory explains that when Aslan said they could never go back to Narnia, he meant the old Narnia. But that was not the *real* Narnia. The old Narnia had a beginning and an end. It was only a shadow, a copy of the real Narnia. In the same way, Digory says, our own world is only a shadow or a copy of something in the real world. All that really matters in the old Narnia is drawn into the new Narnia. Of course this real Narnia *is* different, as different as waking from dreaming.[302]

In this conversation Lewis is echoing Plato's *Allegory of the Cave*. Even Digory, the professor, admits that it is all in Plato. In the *Allegory*, Plato invites us to imagine humanity as dwelling in an underground cave with a long entrance open to the light across the whole width of the cave. Humanity has been in this condition since childhood, with necks and legs chained, so they have to stay where they are. They cannot move their heads around because of the chains so they can only look forward. However, light comes to them from a fire burning behind them, higher up, at a distance. Between the fire and the prisoners is a road above their level, and along the road a low wall has been built, along which puppeteers, as it were, carry various objects. The shadows of these objects are projected by the firelight on to the wall of the cave which is the only thing the prisoners can see. Naturally, the prisoners seeing the shadows of various objects think the shadows are the reality, having lived in this condition all their lives. If someone were to come down into the cave from the world of light and release these prisoners, then the prisoners would be able to turn and slowly begin to take in their real situation. Eventually, upon exiting the cave, the prisoners would even discover what the whole world is like outside of the cave.[303]

---

this life. See Lewis' letter to his friend Sister Penelope of January 10, 1952, in which he requests her prayers for Mrs. Moore who had died the year before. (*Collected Letters*, Volume III, p. 158.)

302 *The Last Battle*, pp. 169-170.

303 Rouse, W. H. D., translator, *Great Dialogues of Plato*, New York: New American Library, 1956, [*The Republic*, Book VII], pp. 312-316.

The final chapter of *The Last Battle* is entitled "Farewell to Shadow-Lands". So clearly in this chapter Lewis is echoing, once again, Plato's *Allegory*. When Tirian and the others go through the stable door it is like Plato's prisoners leaving the cave, they are now entering the real world and not dealing merely with the shadows of reality anymore.

According to Lewis, heaven is the most utterly real place. In *The Great Divorce* Lewis suggests that heaven will be so real that the blades of grass will pierce our feet when we first arrive there; we will have to become more real ourselves, and less ghostly, in order to handle the hard reality of heaven. Heaven is the place where we will become fully human, where we will discover all that we were meant to be.[304] That is why we know so much more about heaven than about hell, because heaven is the home of true humanity.[305] Heaven is the place of joy which cannot be shaken.[306] Heaven will be truly home, as Jewel the unicorn suggests.[307]

As the kings and queens run after Aslan, further up and further in to the new Narnia, eventually they come to a walled garden[308] atop a green hill, and who should meet them at the golden gates but Reepicheep the Talking Mouse! This walled garden is the real twin of the garden Digory and Polly traveled to find in *The Magician's Nephew*; it is paradise regained. Soon Tirian is greeted by his father, the good King Erlian. And inside the walled garden the kings and queens meet all the great Narnians of old. Among them are: Glimfeather and Puddleglum, Rilian and Caspian, Trumpkin and Trufflehunter, Cor and Corin, the Beavers and Mr. Tumnus, King Frank and Queen Helen, the latter couple who are indeed like Adam and Eve from our own world.

As Lucy spends time staring out over the garden, she comes to realize that the garden is like the stable, bigger inside than outside. As she looks even more intently she sees her own England and her mother and father waving at her, like people waving from a ship to people

---
304 See *The Weight of Glory*, p. 119, and *The Problem of Pain*, p. 125.
305 *The Problem of Pain*, p. 127.
306 *The Great Divorce*, p. 108.
307 *The Last Battle*, p. 171.
308 As mentioned in the chapter on *The Magician's Nephew*, the walled garden is a Persian picture of Paradise. Intriguingly, Lewis' *Chronicles* end in a garden, whereas the book of Revelation ends in a city.

waiting to meet them on the dock. Mr. Tumnus tells Lucy that all the real countries are spurs connected to the great mountains of Aslan, thus suggesting that the way to get to her loved ones is through Aslan himself.

Finally, Aslan meets Lucy and the others as he comes leaping down the cliffs at the center of the garden. The Lion tells the kings and queens from our world that indeed, there was a railway accident and that they, along with the Pevensies' father and mother, are dead. School is over; vacation has begun. The nightmare has ended; morning has arrived.

Coming from someone like Lewis who had horrible times at school and even more horrible nightmares throughout his entire life, such language is deeply meaningful. What better way to describe heaven than eternal holiday . . . everlasting morning?

Discussion Questions

1. What parallels do you see between the events in *The Last Battle* and the end-of-the-world events as described in the Bible? Do the early chapters of *The Last Battle* build in you a sense of despair? If so, how?
2. How can we be more like Tirian in facing the possible end of our own world, or at least living for Aslan in our time and place?
3. How did you respond to the dwarfs who refuse to be taken in?
4. What do you think of Lewis' description of the end of Narnia and the final judgment of all its creatures? Does this judgment seem just? Merciful?
5. Did you like the way Lewis brought all the chief characters back together from the earlier Narnia stories? How did you react to Susan not being there?
6. What did you think of Emeth, and Aslan allowing him into the new Narnia? What do you think Lewis is trying to say through this character?
7. How do you respond to the new world(s) described at the end of *The Last Battle*? Do Lewis' descriptions make you want to go there? Why or why not?

Conclusion: How to Live Like a Narnian

Many children of all ages have wanted to live in Narnia after reading C. S. Lewis' wonderful books. On viewing the Lewis family wardrobe, now at Wheaton College in Illinois, some have been disappointed to find they cannot step through that wardrobe into Narnia. However, there are several ways we can all live like Narnians without ever going there.

Enjoy the Beauty of Aslan's Creation

Hopefully this book has reminded you of the beauty of Aslan's creation as described by the artful pen of C. S. Lewis. We have felt the delight of a number of characters in his stories as they have traveled on foot, on horseback, by owl and by ship throughout Lewis' sub-creation. The good news is that we can meet Aslan in our world too, though he goes by another name here. Aslan, the creator of Narnia, and the creator of our world are the same. So one way we can live like Narnians is by enjoying the beauty of creation around us. As Psalm 19 tells us, "The heavens declare the glory of God; the skies proclaim the work of his hands."

C. S. Lewis believed strongly in the importance of spending time outside, in God's creation, every day. He believed that by this practice his soul was renewed. Lewis enjoyed daily walks on the grounds of Magdalen College, Oxford and later Magdalene College, Cambridge. In fact, it was a conversation along Addison's Walk in Oxford which led Lewis back to faith in Christ. During his many years as a fellow and tutor at Oxford he would often take breaks in the middle of the day to go for a walk in the countryside and pray.

Lewis went on yearly walking tours across the English countryside, during his younger years, with his brother and other friends. One of his favorite places to walk, hike really, was in the Malvern Hills near his old prep school, Malvern College. Lewis spent many a holiday in Malvern during his adult years where he often went hiking to the top of the British Camp to enjoy the long views of Wales, on one side, and the Cotswolds, on the other. As mentioned earlier in this book, Lewis also had a life-long love affair with the sea. When he wasn't vacationing in England he would return to his native Ireland where he delighted in walks by the seaside or even a tumble in the surf.

We too can live like Narnians, as C. S. Lewis did, enjoying God's creation around us on a daily basis. Not all of us are blessed to live in the country. But even those of us who live in the city can take time to walk in a park everyday, listen to a bird-song, hear the wind whistle through the trees, and whisper a prayer to our creator. If we would all make this a daily habit, as Lewis did, we might find our souls renewed every day, as his was.

Trust in the Lion of Judah

A second way we can all learn to live like Narnians is by trusting in the Lion of Judah. Lewis makes quite plain the correspondence between Aslan, the Lion who died for the traitor Edmund on the Stone Table, and Jesus as the Lion of Judah who died for sinners on the cross. As the Apostle Paul tells us, "God demonstrates his own love for us in this: While we were still sinners, Christ died for us."[309]

We are all a bit like Edmund in different ways. We all seek to fill some emptiness deep inside our souls with things which just won't satisfy. We spend money for things which are not real spiritual bread and thereby run up a huge tab. We sell our souls, perhaps not to a White Witch, but to many other things and people, and we lose ourselves in the process. Just as Aslan gave his life blood for the life of Edmund and all Narnia to break the spell of the White Witch forever, so Jesus has given his life blood to break the power of sin and Satan and selfishness in our lives. If we learn to trust the one who gave his life for us and put

---

309 Romans 5:8

our lives under his management, then we will taste the sweetness of forgiveness and be living like the best Narnians indeed.

C. S. Lewis put his trust in the crucified one at the age of thirty-three. It took a long time for the witch's enchantment to melt away from his life. However, the transformation was evident to all who knew Jack. The power of Christ to change a person's life is something he never tired of writing about. Even late into his life here on earth Jack was continuing to marvel at the new depths of forgiveness and love he was discovering through his relationship with Jesus Christ.

Discover You are a Child of the King

Shasta did not know he was the child of King Lune of Archenland, but he knew something was missing in his life, so he went searching for that something–to Narnia and the North. Another thing Shasta didn't know was that the something missing was really Someone. He did not discover this great truth until he met Aslan on his early morning walk into Narnia. Discovering that his father was really King Lune, not Arsheesh the fisherman, changed Shasta's life dramatically and permanently. As a child of the King he realized he had undreamed of resources, but also unsought responsibilities–to care for and protect the kingdom of Archenland.

Scripture tells us that we too are children of the King, though many of us do not realize it. We are a chosen people, a royal priesthood, a holy nation, a people belonging to God, that we may declare the praises of him who called us out of darkness into his wonderful light.[310] We have amazing untapped resources at our fingertips. We have a Father who will meet all our needs according to his glorious riches in Christ Jesus.[311] And we also have the responsibility, as sons and daughters of the King, to care for, protect and extend his kingdom by loving the King and loving all of his subjects.

Help Restore the Kingdom

This leads to yet another way we can live like Narnians. That is by restoring the Kingdom to the rightful King, just as the Pevensies

---

310 1 Peter 2:9
311 Philippians 4:19

restored the Kingdom of Narnia to Caspian as the rightful sovereign. Through our examination of *Prince Caspian* we have seen how the Pevensies and the Old Narnians did this. The key factors were the winding of the magic horn, obedience to rightful authority, trust in Aslan, turning away from doubt and human solutions.

In our world we too can be part of the "underground" movement to return the Kingdom of this world to its rightful sovereign–King Jesus. We can do this through prayer, obedience, faith and repentance. Jesus tells us that if we seek first the kingdom of God and his righteousness we will have all needful things added unto us in our fight for the true King.[312]

Grow in Relationship with Aslan

Wouldn't you love to have a relationship with Aslan? I know it might be scary at first to meet him, pretty awesome really. However, once we got over the first-meeting jitters, wouldn't we all want to grow in a relationship with him?

The Voyage of the Dawn Treader shows us just how to do that. We learn about two vital practices from that book. The first one is: reading the wonderful story in the Magician's Book. The second is: eating and drinking at Aslan's Table.

Aslan wants to tell us the wonderful story in our world just as he promised to do for Lucy. We can read that great story every day in the Bible, especially in the Gospels. The Bible is God's story, breathed out by him, and useful for instructing us, showing us where we are wrong when necessary, setting us back on the right path and useful for training us in the practicalities of right living. If we read the great collection of books called the Bible, every day, we will be well-equipped Narnians, ready for every good deed.[313]

The other thing Aslan wants us to do in order to grow in our relationship with him, is to eat from his table. We have the equivalent of Aslan's Table in our world, except here it is called the Lord's Table, or Holy Communion, or the Lord's Supper, or the Eucharist, or the

---

312 Matthew 6:33
313 See 2 Timothy 3:16-17.

Mass. Lewis once said about Holy Communion that he believed the veil between the worlds is nowhere else so thin and permeable to divine operation. Here a hand from the hidden country touches not only our souls but our bodies. Here is big medicine and strong magic.[314] If we want to be touched by Aslan and grow in our relationship with him we can do nothing better than to eat and drink at his table. Jesus said, "Whoever eats my flesh and drinks my blood remains in me, and I in him."[315]

Rescue other Lost Children

A sixth thing we can do to live like Narnians is to rescue other lost children of the King by following Aslan's signs. Rilian had forgotten that he was the son of King Caspian. He had forgotten his true home in Narnia. He thought evil was good and good evil. There was only one hour of the day during which he was sane, and during that hour he was bound to the enchanted silver chair. Thankfully, Aslan commissioned Jill and Eustace to rescue Prince Rilian and bring him home. And Aslan gave Jill signs to follow to help her in this task.

Similarly, there are many people around us in our world who do not realize they are sons and daughters of the King of kings. They are lost in a world where they don't even know what is good or evil anymore. They are like the prodigal son who wandered away from his father's house and wasted his inheritance in wild living.[316] The good news is that lost people are valuable to the King of kings. And he has commissioned us to find his lost children and bring them home. As Jesus commissioned his first disciples so he commissions us:

> Therefore go and make disciples of all nations, baptizing them in the name of the Father and of the Son and of the Holy Spirit, and teaching them to obey everything I have commanded you. And surely I am with you always, to the very end of the age.[317]

We are on a seek-and-save mission. And we have signs given to us in the Bible to tell us how to carry out our mission. The book of Acts in the New Testament is perhaps the best instruction booklet in

---

314 *Letters to Malcolm: Chiefly on Prayer*, p. 103.
315 John 6:56
316 See Luke 15.
317 Matthew 28:19-20

the world about how to find lost people and bring them home to their Father's house.

Fight the Last Battle

Finally, if we are to live like Narnians in our own time and world, we must be ready, like King Tirian, to fight the last battle valiantly, and also be ready to pass through the stable door. Our battle may not be against flesh and blood, as was Tirian's. Therefore we need to put on the spiritual armor of God which includes: the belt of truth, the breastplate of righteousness, shoes ready to run with the good news of Jesus, the shield of faith, the helmet of salvation, and the sword of the Spirit which is the word of God.[318] We need to be ready to face death valiantly, knowing that on the other side of the stable door is Aslan's real Narnia. As the Apostle Paul once said, "To live is Christ, and to die is gain." [319]

Are you longing to enter into the New Narnia, to see Aslan face to face? If so, then I have good news for you. You will get there. As C. S. Lewis once wrote, your soul has a peculiar shape to it because it is made to fit a particular place in heaven. It is not humanity in the abstract that is going to be saved, but you–the individual reader. Your eyes shall behold the real Aslan. All that you are, sins apart, is destined, if you will let Aslan have his way, to find total satisfaction.[320]

---

318 See Ephesians 6:10-20.
319 Philippians 1:21
320 See *The Problem of Pain*, p. 147.

Discussion Questions

1. Which of the seven guidelines for living like a Narnian do you most want to employ in your life at this time? Why?
2. If you could step into any of the Narnia stories which one would it be and why?
3. If you could be any character in any of the Narnia stories, who would you like to be and why?
4. What is your favorite passage in the Narnia books? If you are using this book with a group how about reading your favorite passage aloud to your friends?
5. In what order do you like reading the Narnia stories? Why is that order of reading more meaningful to you?
6. Do you think *The Chronicles of Narnia* present Lewis' theology in story form? Why or why not?
7. What Lewis book would you like to explore next?

Bibliography

Bettelheim, Bruno, *The Uses of Enchantment: The Meaning and Importance of Fairy Tales*, New York: Random House, 1977.

Carpenter, Humphrey, *Tolkien: A Biography*, Boston: Houghton Mifflin Company, 1977.

Craft, Charlotte, *King Midas and the Golden Touch*, New York: William Morrow, 1999.

Green, Roger Lancelyn and Hooper, Walter, *C. S. Lewis: A Biography*, Glasgow: Collins, 1980.

Hooper, Walter, ed., *All My Road Before Me: The Diary of C. S. Lewis, 1922-1927*, San Diego: Harcourt Brace Jovanovich, 1992.

___, ed., *C. S. Lewis: Companion & Guide*, New York: HarperCollins, 1996.

___, ed., *The Collected Letters of C. S. Lewis, Volumes 1-3*, New York: HarperCollins, 2000, 2004, 2007.

___, ed., *They Stand Together: The Letters of C. S. Lewis to Arthur Greeves (1914-1963)*, New York: Macmillan, 1979.

___ and Lewis, W. H., editors. *Letters of C. S. Lewis*, San Diego: Harcourt Brace & Company, 1993.

Kilby, Clyde S., *Images of Salvation*, Wheaton: Harold Shaw Publishers, 1978.

Lewis, C. S., *Christian Reflections*, London: Geoffrey Bles, 1967.

___, *God in the Dock*, Grand Rapids: Eerdmans, 1994.

___, *Letters to an American Lady*, Grand Rapids: Eerdmans, 1967.

___, *Letters to Children*, New York: Macmillan, 1985.

___, *Letters to Malcolm: Chiefly on Prayer*, New York: Harcourt Brace Jovanovich, 1964.

___, *Mere Christianity*, New York: Macmillan, 1984.

___, *Miracles*, New York: Macmillan, 1978.

___, *On Stories: and Other Essays on Literature*, San Diego: Harcourt Brace & Company, 1982.

___, *Present Concerns*, San Diego: Harcourt Brace Jovanovich, 1986.

___, *Prince Caspian*, New York: Macmillan, 1973.

___, *Reflections on the Psalms*, San Diego: Harcourt Brace Jovanovich, 1958.

___, *Surprised by Joy*, New York: Harcourt Brace Jovanovich, 1955.

___, *Studies in Words*, Cambridge: Cambridge University Press, 1991.

___, *That Hideous Strength*, New York: Simon & Schuster, 1996.

___, *The Abolition of Man*, New York: Macmillan, 1978.

___, *The Allegory of Love*, New York: Oxford University Press, 1967.

___, *The Discarded Image*, Cambridge: Cambridge University Press, 1964.

___, *The Four Loves*, San Diego: Harcourt Brace Jovanovich, 1960.

___, *The Great Divorce*, London: Geoffrey Bles, 1945.

___, *The Horse and His Boy*, New York: Macmillan, 1980.

___, *The Last Battle*, New York: Macmillan, 1973.

___, *The Lion, the Witch and the Wardrobe*, New York: Macmillan, 1970.

___, *The Magician's Nephew*, New York: Macmillan, 1973.

___, *The Pilgrim's Regress*, Grand Rapids: Eerdmans, 1981.

___, *The Problem of Pain*, New York: Macmillan, 1986.

___, *The Screwtape Letters*, New York: Macmillan, 1977.

___, *The Silver Chair*, New York: Macmillan, 1973.

___, *The Voyage of the Dawn Treader*, New York: Macmillan, 1962.

___, *The Weight of Glory*, New York: Macmillan, 1980.

___, *The World's Last Night*, San Diego: Harcourt Brace & Company, 1987.

___, *They Asked for a Paper*, London: Geoffrey Bles, 1962.

Rouse, W. H. D., translator, *Great Dialogues of Plato*, New York: New American Library, 1956.

Sayer, George, *Jack: A Life of C. S. Lewis*, Wheaton, Illinois: Crossway, 1994.

Shakespeare, William, *The Tragedy of Macbeth*, New York: The New American Library, 1963.

Vaus, Will, *Mere Theology*, Downers Grove, Il. InterVarsity Press, 2004.

___, *The Professor of Narnia: The C. S. Lewis Story*, Washington, D. C.: Believe Books, 2008.

Watts, Victor, translator, *Boethius: The Consolation of Philosophy*, London: Penguin Books, 1999.

Subject Index

A
Allegory, 3, 114-115, 126
Ascension, 98
Austen, Jane, 18, 59

B
Baptism, 72-73
Beauty, 8, 17, 27, 41, 44-46, 76, 80, 94, 118
Belief, 19, 23, 32, 33, 35, 47, 49, 53, 54-55, 58-65, 67, 72, 77, 81, 82, 92-93, 95, 97, 101, 105, 106, 111, 118, 122
Bettleheim, Bruno, 88
Bible, 77, 93, 121-122
Boethius, 55, 57
Bravery, 24, 40-43, 47, 84, 87, 90

C
Calling, 4, 37, 62, 92
Chaucer, Geoffrey, 94
Chesterton, G. K., 57
Church, 22, 34, 61, 64-65, 72
Communion, 72, 81-82, 121-122,
Confession, 20, 31
Conscience, 7, 14-15, 25-26, 42, 102
Conversion, 4, 29, 37-52, 70, 73
Creation, 7-10, 18, 20, 23, 27, 36, 44, 62, 65-67, 98, 111, 118-119

D
Dance, the Great, 62
Death, 27, 32-34, 39, 69, 71, 75, 84, 88, 98, 99, 106, 123
Discipline, 40, 70, 81
Doubt, 63, 67, 84, 121

E
Eliot, T. S., 77
Environmentalism, 66
Evangelism, 62-63, 92
Evolution, 10

F
Faith, faithfulness, 9, 29, 37, 47, 60-63, 70, 95, 97, 110, 113, 118, 119-120, 121, 123
Fall, the, 11, 13, 27, 64
Foreknowledge, 20, 55
Forgiveness, 20, 106, 120
Freedom, 26, 33, 39-41, 54-55, 62, 96, 98

G
Glorification, 21
Gresham, Douglas, 1, 34, 129

H
Heaven, 57, 61, 71, 74, 82-84, 98, 107, 115-116, 123
Hell, 57, 71, 83, 110, 115
Herbert, George, 57
Hierarchy, 46-47, 58
Holiness, 30-31, 48, 57, 82, 99, 120
Holy Spirit, the, 34, 90, 106, 122
Homeliness, 18
Honesty, 42
Hooper, Walter, 2, 4, 45, 70, 77, 88, 125, 128
Humility, 16-17, 18, 34-35, 42-44, 47

I
Identity, 34, 39-40, 92
Incarnation, 64

J
Jenkins, Anne (Waller), i-ii, 4, 102
Johnson, Samuel, 57
Journey, 13, 32, 38-42, 68-70, 73, 78, 82-84
Joy, 8, 24, 37-38, 41, 49, 63, 69, 115
Judgment, 65, 81, 110-113
Julian of Norwich, 23
Justification, 21

K
Kilby, Clyde S., 34, 128
Kingship, 16, 34-35, 39, 41, 46-49, 58, 61, 62, 65, 75, 87, 111, 120

L
Lewis, Albert, 88
Lewis, C. S., writings,
  All My Road Before Me, 70
  Christian Reflections, 97
  Collected Letters, 4, 114
  God in the Dock, 65, 66, 81
  Letters of C. S. Lewis, 2, 10, 18, 23
  Letters to an American Lady, 84
  Letters to Children, 3, 4, 5, 10, 34, 82-83, 109
  Letters to Malcolm: Chiefly on Prayer, 28, 82, 122
  Mere Christianity, 15, 16, 19-22, 26, 29-30, 32, 54, 55, 72, 84, 106, 113
  Miracles, 33, 35, 95
  On Stories, 2, 88
  Present Concerns, 17
  Prince Caspian, 4, 53-66, 89, 90, 100, 121
  Reflections on the Psalms, 10, 55, 56, 77
  Studies in Words, 15
  Surprised by Joy, 18, 37, 70-71, 88
  That Hideous Strength, 65-66
  The Abolition of Man, 10, 60, 97
  The Allegory of Love, 3
  The Discarded Image, 55
  The Four Loves, 21
  The Great Divorce, 71, 83, 110, 115
  The Horse and His Boy, 4, 37-51, 68, 89, 90
  The Last Battle, 4, 56, 89, 90, 99, 100, 102-116, 123
  The Lion, the Witch and the Wardrobe, 1, 2, 4, 5, 20, 24-35, 53, 54, 90, 100, 104, 128
  The Magician's Nephew, 4, 5, 7-22, 25, 53, 90, 115
  The Pilgrim's Regress, 3, 24, 29,38, 83
  The Problem of Pain, 8, 10, 25, 49, 50, 104, 115, 123
  The Screwtape Letters, 65
  The Silver Chair, i, 4, 87-100
  The Voyage of the Dawn Treader, 4, 68-85, 89, 121
  The Weight of Glory, 18, 25, 57, 64, 82, 84, 97-98, 115
  The World's Last Night, 61
  They Asked for a Paper, 59
  They Stand Together, 45
Lewis, Flora, 45, 88
Lewis, Warren, 45, 88
Logic, 4, 29-30
Longfellow, Henry Wadsworth, 37
Love, 3, 17-18, 19, 21, 33, 78, 111, 116, 119, 120

M
MacDonald, George, 57, 71, 110
Magic, 7, 8, 12, 15, 20, 23, 24, 27, 32, 60, 61, 75-77, 89, 98, 121, 122
Midas, King, 75
Moore, Janie King, 113-114
Morality, 7-8, 20, 25-26, 41, 60

N
New Jerusalem, 83, 107
Nobility, 47
Northernness, 37-38, 41, 45, 46, 120
Nostalgia, 56-57
Numinous, the, 8, 24-25, 36

O
Old Western Man, 59-60
Otto, Rudolf, 57
Oxford, 2, 46, 66, 97, 118

P
Plato, 55-56, 114-115
Postmodernism, 96-97
Prayer, 28, 31, 32, 54, 60-61, 70, 77, 78-79, 113, 114, 118-119, 121

Pride, 15-16, 41-43, 49, 65
Providence, 50-51, 94-95
Psychology, 79, 87
Purgatory, 83
R
Regeneration, 33-34
Repentance, 20, 49, 63, 121
Resurrection, 4, 24, 33-34, 61, 64, 98, 99

S
Satan, 11, 13, 27, 34, 65, 74, 94, 98, 103, 105, 119
Sayer, George, 45-46, 88
School, 29, 37, 45, 87-89, 116, 119
Second Coming, 64, 107
Sehnsucht, 24, 37-38, 56
Self-centered, Selfishness, 17-18, 27, 33, 41-44, 70-71, 102, 110, 119
Shakespeare, William, 65
Slavery, 39-41, 68-69, 83, 96, 98
Sovereignty, 33, 55, 66, 104, 121

T
Tao, the, 7, 13-15, 19-20, 26, 60
Temptation, 11-13, 23, 25, 27-28, 36, 77, 97
Time, 53-56, 59-60, 110, 112
Tolkien, J.R.R., 34, 46, 66
Trilemma, 29
Trinity, 30, 48, 62
Truth, 9, 12, 20, 29, 32, 61, **91**, 97, 105, 106, 111, 112, 123

V
Values, 41-44, 97
Vanity, 16, 43,
Vice, 15, 17, 43, 101
Virgil, 57
Virtue, 15, 18, 43, 95, 101

W
Wagner, Richard, 12, 38
Warfare, 4, 34-35, 42, 43, 58, 64-65, 74, 79, 87-100, 106-107
Williams, Charles, 57
Wordsworth, William, 57

Scripture Index

Genesis
1:28-2:16, *10, 66*
2:7, *10, 90*
2:9, *11*
2:17, *10, 11, 12*
3:1-24, *11, 98*
3:8, *12*
7:2-3, *9*
19:27, *60*
20:5-6, *26*
Exodus
20, *14*
24:4, *60*
32, *93*
34:4, *60*
Numbers
32:23, *20*

Deuteronomy
5, *14*
6:6-7, *93*
Joshua
1-24, *64*
1:9, *79*
Judges
5:19, *107*
1 Samuel
1:19, *60*
24:5, *25*
25:31, *26*
2 Samuel
24:10, *25*
1 Kings
19, *48*

2 Kings
23:29, *107*
2 Chronicles
35:22, *107*
Job
1:5, *60*
27:6, *26*
32:8, *90*
38:6-7, *8*
42:1-6, *21*
Psalms
5:3, *60*
19, *118*
33:6, *90*
90:4, *55*
116:15, *99*
139:16, *21*
Proverbs
25:11, *12*
25:25, *38*
28:13, *20*
Isaiah
6:1-5, *30, 48, 99*
13:10, *110*
14:12, *11*
27:1, *74*
34:4, *110*
55:8, *61*
57:16, *99*
Jeremiah
2:13, *91*
Ezekiel
36:26, *33*
37:5-6, *90*
Joel
2:30-31, *112*
Matthew
4:1-11, *13, 74, 94*
6:33, *121*
8:23-27, *69*
10:29, *95*
18:3, *61, 62*

24:29, *110*
25:14-30, *110*
25:31-46, *111, 113*
26:29, *82*
27:51, *98*
28:19-20, *21, 48, 122*
Mark
1:35, *60*
3:20-30, *98, 106*
8:22-26, *63*
9:2-29, *93*
10:45, *35, 47*
13:5, *103*
Luke
5:1-11, *21*
15, *92, 122*
19:11-27, *110*
24:36-43, *33*
John
1:29, *85*
3:16, *111-112*
4:10, *91*
4:14, *91*
6:37, *44, 92*
6:56, *122*
10:1, *12*
12:46, *79*
14:6, *91*
20:22, *34*
20:24-29, *63*
21, *85*
Acts
1-28, *122*
2:1-4, *9*
2:19-20, *112*
4:12, *91*
13:2, *90*
23:1, *26*
24:16, *26*
26:18, *79*
Romans
2:14-15, *14*

3:10-11, *33*
5:3-4, *70*
5:8, *119*
6:16-17, *69*
8:18-25, *62, 98*
8:29-30, *21*
9:1, *26*
13:5, *26*
1 Corinthians
4:4, *26*
11:27-32, *81*
2 Corinthians
1:12, *26*
4:6, *79*
11:14-15, *27, 94*
Ephesians
2:6, *35*
4:8, *98*
5:8, *79*
6:10-20, *123*
6:17, *13, 94*
Philippians
1:21, *123*
4:19, *120*
Colossians
1:13, *79*
2 Thessalonians
2:1-12, *103*
1 Timothy
1:19, *26*
4:2, *15*
2 Timothy
1:3, *26*
3:16-17, *121*
Hebrews
4:14, *85*
4:15, *21*
9:9, *26*
10:22, *26*
11:3, *9*
13:18, *26*

James
1:14, *12, 27*
4:4, *58*
4:7, *74*
1 Peter
1:2, *21*
2:9, *79, 120*
3:16, 21, *26*
4:12-13, *69*
5:8-9, *74, 94*
2 Peter
3:7, *12, 112*
3:8, *55*
3:10, *112*
1 John
2:15-17, *75*
2:18, *102*
2:22, *102*
4:3, *102*
2 John
1:7, *103*
Revelation
5:5, *85*
12:7-17, *11*
12:9, *74*
13, *103*
16:13, *103*
16:14, *16, 107*
19:11-21, *107*
19:20, *103*
20:1-3, *98*
20:7-10, *107*
20:10, *103*
21, *83*
21:1-3, *107*
22:2, *108*
21-22, *115*

Acknowledgements

First, last and always my heart is filled with thanksgiving for my family. The boys to whom I read the Narnia books while living in Ireland are growing so fast, they have perhaps reached that in-between age where fairy tales do not hold for them the same magic they once did. However, it is my hope that as adults they will one day return to Narnia and discover many spiritual jewels buried in the ancient treasure chamber there. And perhaps if they do get back to Narnia, this book their father labored over in love will be of some assistance in unlocking the door to the treasure house.

Of course my wife Becky deserves "the Lion's share" of my love. Her support for my writing and her constant encouragement are beyond valuation.

I am grateful to Ted Baehr for permission to reprint the chapter in this book on *The Lion, the Witch and the Wardrobe* (in a slightly altered form) which was originally written for his book, *Narnia Beckons*. Thanks to Ted for that invitation way back in 2004 which got me thinking and writing on this topic of the spiritual themes in the Narnia books.

Thanks to all those folks who have patiently listened to me speak about the spiritual themes in Narnia over the past few years. Your wise and discerning responses have certainly shaped my ongoing thinking on this topic.

Though I purposely did not read any of the secondary works on Narnia while I was writing this book, I am nonetheless in debt to some of the first "Narnia scholars" who touched on this subject in their writing. I think especially of Walter Hooper and his classic book *Past Watchful Dragons*, soon to be re-issued, I hope, in an updated version. I also wish to acknowledge the late Clyde Kilby, whose book *Images of Salvation* first got me thinking more deeply about the spiritual themes in Lewis' fiction.

Another great contribution to Narnia studies has been Michael Ward's *Planet Narnia*. Whatever one thinks of Ward's thesis, there is no doubt that his book masterfully leads us "further up and further in" to Lewis' medievalism. My book was actually written before *Planet Narnia* appeared and so, unfortunately, does not engage its excellent points. Rather than seeing them as competing themes I think it is possible, if one accepts Ward's thesis, to view the planetary and spiritual themes as overlapping in the Narnia books.

Thanks also are due to Doug and Merrie Gresham who graciously accommodated us at Rathvinden House for much of 2004. Without the leisure of that time and the inspiration of the green hills of Ireland, this book might never have been conceived.

My deep appreciation is extended to Robert Trexler of Winged Lion Press for seeing in my manuscript something worthy of publication and a valued addition to "Narnia studies." It is my hope and prayer that Winged Lion will have a long life of introducing many readers to great works of literature, Lewis' and others.

Finally, whenever I think of Narnia, I can't help but think of my fourth grade teacher, Mrs. Ewing, who first opened the wardrobe door for me. I hope that wherever you are, Mrs. E., that you know what a life-changing difference you made in the life of at least one of your students. Maybe someday we will meet again, if not here, then in the new Narnia. Until then, may Aslan's blessings be upon you.

Other Titles of Interest

C. S. Lewis

C. S. Lewis: Views From Wake Forest - Essays on C. S. Lewis
Michael Travers, editor

Contains sixteen scholarly presentations from the international C. S. Lewis convention in Wake Forest, NC. Walter Hooper shares his important essay "Editing C. S. Lewis," a chronicle of publishing decisions after Lewis' death in 1963.

"*Scholars from a variety of disciplines address a wide range of issues. The happy result is a fresh and expansive view of an author who well deserves this kind of thoughtful attention.*"
                Diana Pavlac Glyer, author of *The Company They Keep*

The Hidden Story of Narnia: A Book-By-Book Guide to Lewis' Spiritual Themes
Will Vaus

A book of insightful commentary – Will Vaus points out connections between the *Narnia* books and spiritual and biblical themes in our world, as well as between ideas in the *Narnia* books and C. S. Lewis' other books. Each chapter includes questions for individual use or small group discussion.

C. S. Lewis & Philosophy as a Way of Life: His Philosophical Thoughts
Adam Barkman

C. S. Lewis is rarely thought of as a "philosopher" per se despite having both studied and taught philosophy for several years at Oxford. Lewis's long journey to Christianity was essentially philosophical – passing through seven different stages. This 624 page book is an invaluable reference for C. S. Lewis scholars and fans alike.

C. S. Lewis: His Literary Achievement
Colin Manlove

"This is a positively brilliant book, written with splendor, elegance, profundity and evidencing an enormous amount of learning. This is probably not a book to give a first-time reader of Lewis. But for those who are more broadly read in the Lewis corpus this book is an absolute gold mine of information. The author gives us a magnificent overview of Lewis' many writings, tracing for us thoughts and ideas which recur throughout, and at the same time telling us how each book differs from the others. I think it is not extravagant to call *C. S. Lewis: His Literary Achievement* a *tour de force*."
                Robert Merchant, *St. Austin Review*, Book Review Editor

George MacDonald

Diary of an Old Soul & The White Page Poems
George MacDonald and Betty Aberlin

The first edition of George MacDonald's book of daily poems included a blank page opposite each page of poems. Readers were invited to write their own reflections on the "white page." MacDonald wrote: "Let your white page be ground, my print be seed, growing to golden ears, that faith and hope may feed." Betty Aberlin responded to MacDonald's invitation with daily poems of her own.

Betty Aberlin's close readings of George MacDonald's verses and her thoughtful responses to them speak clearly of her poetic gifts and spiritual intelligence.   Luci Shaw, poet

George MacDonald: Literary Heritage and Heirs
Roderick McGillis, editor

This latest collection of 14 essays sets a new standard that will influence MacDonald studies for many more years. George MacDonald experts are increasingly evaluating his entire corpus within the nineteenth century context.

This comprehensive collection represents the best of contemporary scholarship on George MacDonald. Rolland Hein, author of *George MacDonald: Victorian Mythmaker.*

In the Near Loss of Everything: George MacDonald's Son in America
Dale Wayne Slusser

In the summer of 1887, George MacDonald's son Ronald, newly engaged to artist Louise Blandy, sailed from England to America to teach school. The next summer he returned to England to marry Louise and bring her back to America. On August 27, 1890, Louise died leaving him with an infant daughter. Ronald once described losing a beloved spouse as "the near loss of everything". Dale Wayne Slusser unfolds this poignant story with unpublished letters and photos that give readers a glimpse into the close-knit MacDonald family. Also included is Ronald's essay about his father, *George MacDonald: A Personal Note*, plus a selection from Ronald's 1922 fable, *The Laughing Elf*, about the necessity of both sorrow and joy in life.

A Novel Pulpit: Sermons From George MacDonald's Fiction
David L. Neuhouser

"In MacDonald's novels, the Christian teaching emerges out of the characters and story line, the narrator's comments, and inclusion of sermons given by the fictional preachers. The sermons in the novels are shorter than the ones in collections of MacDonald's sermons and so are perhaps more accessible for some. In any case, they are both stimulating and thought-provoking. This collection of sermons from ten novels serve to bring out the 'freshness and brilliance' of MacDonald's message."

from the author's introduction

Other Titles

To Love Another Person: A Spiritual Journey Through Les Miserables
John Morrison

The powerful story of Jean Valjean's redemption is beloved by readers and theater goers everywhere. In this companion and guide to Victor Hugo's masterpiece, author John Morrison unfolds the spiritual depth and breadth of this classic novel and broadway musical.

The Eye of the Beholder: How to See the World Like a Romantic Poet
Louis Markos

This accessible guide to Romantic poetry focuses almost exclusively on short lyrical poems (the exceptions are Coleridge's *Rime of the Ancient Mariner*, Blake's *Marriage of Heaven and Hell* and Wordsworth's "Preface to Lyrical Ballads"). A detailed bibliographic essay on each poet is provided that cites critical studies of their work.

Through Common Things: Philosophical Reflections on Popular Culture
Adam Barkman

"Barkman presents us with an amazingly wide-ranging collection of philosophical reflections grounded in the everyday things of popular culture – past and present, eastern and western, factual and fictional. Throughout his encounters with often surprising subject-matter (the value of darkness?), he writes clearly and concisely, moving seamlessly between Aristotle and anime, Lord Buddha and Lord Voldemort. . . . This is an informative and entertaining book to read!"
Doug Blomberg, Professor of Philosophy, Institute for Christian Studies

The Order of Harry Potter: The Literary Skill of the Hogwarts Epic
Colin Manlove

The *Harry Potter* stories work as the best kinds of literature work, with the style both mirroring and commenting on the content. *The Order of Harry Potter* book is about their character, their individuality, and how they work as unique forms of literature. It looks at the ways in which they are like and unlike the fantasy works of the 'Inklings'; at their readability; at their treatment of the topic of imagination; at their skill in organization and the use of language; and at their underlying motifs and themes. In other words, it looks at how the books *exist*, rather than what they are *for*.

For these books not only *mean*, they *are*, and what they are is a construct of style and imagery and brilliant invention. Almost without exception literary criticism of the *Harry Potter* books has concerned what they signify: what are their moral, religious or philosophical meanings. In moving away from such readings Colin Manlove brings the debate back to where it should start, from a discussion of how well the books work. For that, given the millions of their readers who cannot put them down, is the first consideration.

adapted from the author's preface

Will Vaus

- was born outside of New York City and grew up in Southern California.
- is the son of Jim Vaus, former organized crime wiretapper who came to Christ through the ministry of Billy Graham in 1949.
- holds a Bachelor of Arts degree in drama from the University of California at San Diego and a Master of Divinity degree from Princeton Theological Seminary.
- has served as a pastor in California, South Carolina and Pennsylvania.
- is the President of Will Vaus Ministries, through which he has communicated the love of Christ around the world since 1988.
- is the author of *Mere Theology: A Guide to the Thought of C. S. Lewis*, *My Father Was a Gangster: The Jim Vaus Story*, and *The Professor of Narnia: The C. S. Lewis Story*.
- and his wife, Becky, have been married since 1988 and have three sons: James, Jonathan and Joshua.
- has a website you can visit: www.willvaus.com

www.ingramcontent.com/pod-product-compliance
Lightning Source LLC
Chambersburg PA
CBHW030327080526
44584CB00012B/745